JEAN-LOUIS DENIOT INTERIORS

JEAN-LOUIS DENIOT INTERIORS

By DIANE DORRANS SAEKS

Photography by Xavier Béjot
Art direction by Paul McKevitt, Subtitle

RIZZOLI
NEW YORK

New York · Paris · London · Milan

ITHACA

As you set out on the way to Ithaca
Hope that the road is a long one,
Filled with adventures, filled with discoveries…
May you stop at Phoenician trading posts
And there acquire the finest wares:
Mother-of-pearl and coral and amber and ebony;
And heady perfumes of every kind.
Always in your mind keep Ithaca.
To arrive here is your destiny.

— C.P. Cavafy, translated by Daniel Mendelsohn

First published in the United States of America in 2014
by Rizzoli International Publications, Inc.
300 Park Avenue South
New York, NY 10010
www.rizzoliusa.com

© 2014 by Diane Dorrans Saeks
Photographs © 2014 by Xavier Béjot
Photographs on pages 254–67 © 2014 by Jonny Valiant
Photographs on pages 268–81 © 2014 by John Coolidge

2014 2015 2016 2017 / 10 9 8 7 6 5 4 3 2 1

Distributed in the U.S. trade by Random House, New York

Printed in China

ISBN-13: 978-0-8478-4332-9

Library of Congress Control Number: 2014934245

CONTENTS

INTRODUCTION
BY DIANE DORRANS SAEKS

I always want to get as far as possible from the white box," states international architect/interior designer Jean-Louis Deniot. "My interiors are about atmosphere, character, texture, and a sense of harmony, inevitability."

"The source of the decor we create is always a story board, which lays out a scenario, writes a script, and plans the components of a room, its style, and the ultimate goal of the completed architecture and decor," says Paris-based Deniot. "The initial plans are the source for everything that follows. The design is cohesive from the start."

For Deniot, creating a complex and cohesive design means perfecting the interior architecture first. Doors must be correctly aligned and of the right proportions. Ceiling height must be optimum. A fireplace is designed to give a room a sense of stature and focus.

"When I plan interior architecture, I'm thinking about movement around a room, its use and function, and an ideal floor plan," says the designer. "At the same time, I'm envisioning the ambiance, the mood, colors, placement. I take into account the comfort and pleasure of the family, the people who will live there. I consider the location of the building, sunlight, and views. Planning all these components, the decor and furnishings, I leave room for some eccentricity. I like to create a link to the past, and to include concepts that will be unique to that residence. I want a sense of delight, grace. It's all in my head from the first drawings. In the end, I want it to look effortless."

In 2000, with his prized architecture diploma from the École Camondo in hand, Jean-Louis Deniot launched Cabinet Jean-Louis Deniot in a tiny office on rue Vaneau in Paris. Two years later his office, now managed by his sister, Virginie, expanded to rue de l'Université, and soon after to the quiet and discreetly hidden rue de Verneuil on the Left Bank among antique dealers and leading art galleries.

"I studied architecture for two years, and then it was five years at Camondo," he recalls. "It was a very rigorous contemporary architecture program, and students had to produce the most advanced concepts. I found it interesting but they were teaching only two hours of art and architecture history. Far from enough. So I studied and researched on my own. I did it in private, scared to be pointed at as a retro, a neo, a would-be architect who delved into history."

Deniot's enterprise and intense private studies, and his inventive solution, became emblematic of his highly successful professional life. He learned and drew strictly contemporary and modern architecture at school. In a city steeped in architectural riches, the eighteenth century did not exist for that program. So to feed his soul, Deniot made the study of design and architecture his mission, his passion. It remains a source of pleasure and professionalism to this day.

"I love the purity of modernism, but I appreciate also the two previous millennia of architecture. It was so ironic that as a classicist, I felt like a rebel," said Deniot. "But it was obvious that when you graduate from school, nobody is hiring you to come out with weird concepts. They hire you because you know how to make a Louis XVI apartment. I was emulating Le Corbusier for school. I was also studying Palladio, the Directoire period, everything in the eighteenth century, and the classicism of Ledoux and Arbus—all of which still inspire me today."

Upon graduation he already had design clients. Even then, he refused to work for just anyone. "I promised myself never to take clients I did not really want to work with," he says. "I thought I would prefer to eat just bread than have a horrible client. Thank goodness clients immediately came along, because I hate bread."

Deniot was the only one of his classmates able to open his firm just after graduation precisely because of his love of classicism. This passion for and practice of classicism, so pure and harmonious, so timeless, has been iconic for his career.

I first met Jean-Louis Deniot soon after he opened his office. I'd been invited by longtime friends to attend the Prix de Diane thoroughbred horse races at Chantilly. We stopped for lunch at a nearby country residence that Deniot was renovating, for which he had designed enchanting interiors. Some of them are in this book.

In just a few fast years, Deniot became the young superstar on the Paris scene. Then in Los Angeles and New York, he gathered a dazzling roster of worldly clients, mostly by quiet reference from one client to another—an ideal introduction. Deniot, with great discretion, appeals to discerning connoisseurs, style-conscious executives, Old Guard Parisians, chic young London couples, high-flying art collectors, and clients in India, Capri, Monte Carlo, Colombia, New York, Chicago, Los Angeles, Kiev, London, and all points north and west. No names or specifics are ever discussed, and his projects are always highly confidential.

Cabinet Jean-Louis Deniot currently employs a team of twenty and sometimes more for special projects, including technicians, and art and antique specialists. "I have a great team in Paris," says Deniot. "As I take on more clients, in India or Morocco or Belgravia, we are bursting at the seams, even though we just added a floor. We like our atelier on rue de Verneuil. Many of my staff have been with me almost from the beginning. There is an architecture department, incredibly fine. I have an excellent design and resources department. I have great resources for antiques and art. And I'm situated on the Left Bank, surrounded by museums, historic edifices, and the top antique dealers, art galleries, fabric showrooms, workshops, and experts in many design fields."

A versatile client meeting room at the Jean-Louis Deniot office in Paris.

Jean-Louis Deniot often cites the designers Henri Samuel and Alberto Pinto as inspiration. "For these masters, the background was never ignored and was never secondary," says Deniot. "Their rooms were cohesive, with every element building the scene, the mood, the visual delight, the feeling, the balance. There was always a direct relationship between the architecture and the decor from the start of a project, from its conception. I work in the same way. Interior architecture comes first."

The designer observes the work of contemporary designers who exhibit a variety of styles with an appraising admiration.

Deniot also admires Adolf Loos for "exactitude," Jean-Michel Frank for his "perfection," Dorothy Draper for "the theatrical side to her design," Renzo Mongiardino for his "collector's spirit and theatricality," and Peter Marino for "couture-style luxury."

"I gather information and inspiration for my designs by osmosis," says Deniot. "We never do historical reconstructions or a total look. We take the major themes of our decoration from the Directoire period up to the 1960s, and update them, simplify them, mix them up. We make a big effort to make our effort go unnoticed. It is the art of being invisible."

Even though he enthusiastically works in many styles, Jean-Louis Deniot's personal preference veers toward a neoclassical style, purified and somewhat monochromatic in the spirit of Jean-Michel Frank.

It's significant that he holds Jean-Michel Frank in such high esteem and occasionally pays homage with such materials as mica and straw marquetry. "For Jean-Michel Frank, luxury was in simplicity. Simplicity dictated the forms and substance of his luxury. He loved the unobtrusiveness of true elegance," said Jean Cocteau, and the same could be said of Deniot.

His interiors are an eclectic assemblage, but the threads, thoughts, and information come together in a cohesive, harmonious room. "I want to achieve a point of equilibrium where the materials, the scale, the colors, the proportions, the volume, light and shade, and a degree of contrast are in balance," says Deniot. "I want the rooms to look alluring or calm during the day, and to have mystery at night, a different mood. And I never want the family who lives there to have any idea how much work it was."

For Deniot, more than 80 percent of creating a new Paris apartment or Los Angeles house is the renovation, which will involve creating a new floor plan, moving and enlarging doors, adding paneling and new interior architecture, moving walls, shaping new rooms, adding architectural details, or installing a new floor. Some apartments he has remodeled in Paris or New York are completely brand new, he notes, from the parquet floors (installed to look original) to the architectural details.

"Often I don't even focus on or discuss the decor until the restoration and remodeling are well under control," he says. "The architecture must be perfect. The placement must be practical and functional. It must have logic. I like the idea that when clients arrive from a trip or from their other houses around the world, everything is in the right place. It is beautiful and totally thought out for them. The kitchen is easy to negotiate, and the sitting room has wonderful sofas and chairs for them and their friends. Children have everything they need.

An apartment in Chicago recently remodeled by Jean-Louis Deniot.

"Sometimes we don't talk about the decor until perhaps a year after we start demolition," says the designer. "We don't necessarily see the clients often. We discuss everything at the beginning and I listen carefully. That's my system. But generally I can achieve a project with four or five meetings. We present the plans and elevations. I want to create something very fresh for them and original, with very evolved concepts."

Subsequently, when the plans, renovations, and concepts have been approved, Deniot says he dives right in. "With a renovation or new construction, I work on the rawest bone of architecture, the skeleton, and make it perfect before proceeding with the millwork, heating, finishes, security systems, sound, and light," says the architect. "All of the inner workings must be invisible and cohesive with the interior."

After the start, his clients can focus on decor. "I don't burden them with every detail or every centimeter. I present very evolved and specific color schemes, fabrics, materials that are cohesive. The concepts are very clear. We make a 'catalog' of choices, all pre-selected, for lighting, case goods, custom pieces, seating, accessories. We narrow it down, make the selections logical and clear. I don't overwhelm my clients. It's efficient, calm."

Deniot notes that he is hired to bring his clients' experience and comfort to a higher level. "As an architect and designer, I don't give them simply what they wish. I think way above. I surprise them," he says. "The decor is designed without trendiness, to last for many years."

In a luxurious house or apartment, says Deniot, everything is in the right place. There are enfilades of rooms that open into one another. Coming and going or being in a room is graceful, easy, and elegant. Everything is thought out for privacy, individual desires, and pleasure. That's luxury.

"Luxury is when it seems flawless, when you reach the right balance between all elements. You cannot give as much importance to all elements, as some need to create the excitement and some just need to be quiet. Luxury is having perfect lighting and beautiful contrasts in selected materials, such as black mother-of-pearl against burlap or fine marble with sisal. I like the juxtaposition of silk velvet and brushed oak, or raw rock crystal with straw marquetry with raw iron or steel on a handwoven silk Nepalese carpet. Understated theatricality—that is what my luxury is about.

"My clients want a sense of history and style throughout a Paris apartment, or a Beverly Hills residence," says Deniot. "They prefer to decorate in a twentieth-century style, but with a sense that the collection has been gathered over years, not months."

"My style is full of history and references coming from many different periods. I like emblematic interiors, full of archetypical furniture one could consider 'cool classical,'" says the designer. This ranges from neoclassical to the 1930s, '40s, '50s, '60s, and '70s. The decor is never literal and never features period styling. It's eclectic and very architectural, with mixed influences, and always focusing on the highest possible level of quality.

"I don't do pure contemporary, as in my mind, it has no soul," says Deniot. " I need to have history in my work."

While he can do a pared-down decor for a house on Capri, minimalism is not for him, but neither is grandiloquence. It is always about balance. "The one constant in my work is the search for harmony and balance, often reflected through symmetry and clearly expressed sightlines. I like the design to be legible," he notes.

His approach refers to French historical precedents, but with American-style comfort to soothe the architecture. For example, nothing gives Jean-Louis more pleasure than creating a statuario marble or mother-of-pearl bathroom, or custom designing a bookcase in bronze and parchment, or large double doors with malachite cladding. He recently completed an office in palm-tree paneling, and in New York he designed eighteen-foot-tall natural linen curtains with poetic hand embroidery in bronze. However, the decor is always well controlled and meticulously balanced. Embellishments must be justified and planned with impeccable precision.

In the matter of color, Jean-Louis Deniot prefers using the subtlest colors and softly muted tones, and featuring custom-mixed glazes in green-white, broken white, chalk, ivory, parchment, and raffia. However, never white walls. "It is the color of plaster. Nothing moves on white, and on it, all seems to be levitating," says Deniot, who finds white too obvious, too stark, tiring.

Artful lighting is central to his work. "I take such care with lighting as it provides the finishing touch. It can improve everything or ruin it all." His principle to this dilemma is simple: "Have at least eight points of light in each room."

Deniot, following inspiration by such 1930s French practitioners as Èmile-Jacques Ruhlmann and Jean-Michel Frank, specifies custom furniture and accessories featuring opaline, bronze, and shagreen, as well as other rare materials that he has resourced for projects. In Paris, he works with devoted craftsmen who continue to nourish these old ways. A new furniture line in his name was launched in 2008, available through the company Collection Pierre. He also designs for such notable French companies as Pouenat and Jean de Merry.

His projects in process include private properties as well as commercial spaces all over the world, including Capri, Colombia, Beverly Hills, the Hamptons, and Moscow, to name a few. He notes that even working long-distance for clients in Kiev, Miami, or Delhi, he can be in close touch, updating them through CAD folders and sites his office sets up. Skype is effective. Emails and videos are brief. Information is very accessible and current. There are no surprises. Distances don't matter.

Like the architecture student who, with spirit and humor defied his professors, he takes joy in new challenges, starts fresh with each project, and even when faced with construction delays in Tangier or late deliveries in Chandigarh, finds delight and passion in his clients, and is energized by process and results.

Deniot recently sent me a message after returning from India: "In Paris now. Have been for the last three weeks on a crazy set of trips ... Moscow, New York, Ukraine, Istanbul, and Delhi, with Paris between each trip. Fun tho! In Delhi last Sunday we set up the townhouse for a shoot. What was quite amazing is that I also stayed at the estate for the first time after five years of construction. I could not believe how beautiful it was. So magical." ∎

LEFT BANK

On autumn evenings, or fresh spring mornings, few excursions offer more pleasure to a design and antiques enthusiast than a quiet Paris meander along narrow rue de Seine and into rue Jacob. With a quick detour around place Furstenburg to peer into fabric showroom windows, a local will take the side entrance into Eglise Saint-Germain-des-Prés to offer a fervent hope and prayer before meeting a dear friend at Café les Deux-Magots to watch the chic and the mondaine saunter past. It's in this insistently romantic quartier, among the bookshops, galleries, and antiquaries, that Jean-Louis Deniot has situated his office. It's among the art schools and university that he finds twentieth-century treasure for his interiors.

PORTRAIT IN TONES OF GRAY

A n observant flâneur walking along rue de Lille just across the Seine from the Louvre might glance up at an eighteenth-century stone apartment building of elegant mien. A shimmer of sunlight strikes its tall windows, and visible just behind the glass are voluptuous folds of raw silk curtains the color of moonlight. The building is indeed handsome and worth a pause on this quiet street. Hidden behind an obscure door on the second floor is the private domain of Jean-Louis Deniot.

The Left Bank building was constructed in the eighteenth century, though some properties nearby have fifteenth- or sixteenth-century foundations and stonework. The 1,200-square-foot apartment is within sound of the bells of Saint-Germain-des-Prés.

Rue de Lille (Karl Lagerfeld's exalted bookshop is at number 7) is rather hidden and villagelike, frequented mainly by chic locals, University of Paris–Sorbonne professors, and trend-setting *galleristes* who visit the smart cafes and artisan cheese or chocolate shops.

The contrast of graphic art and pristine gray and white decor in the entry of the Left Bank apartment sets the tone. Walls and crown moldings were painted in a faux marbre finish to match the floor, designed in a constructivist pattern with Carrara and Statuario marble. The black and white photograph is by Valérie Belin. The bench is part of Deniot's collection for Pouenat, and the bronze mirror is by Hervé Van der Straeten. The ceramic and bronze lamp by Stiffel is from 1stdibs.com. The polygon sculpture in black lacquered finish is from On Site Antiques, Paris. The sleek, modern 1960s sideboard designed by art-inspired Danish furniture designer Finn Juhl was made by master cabinetmaker Niels Vodder and purchased in Brussels. The 1990s limestone sculpture by Philippe Angot is from On Site Antiques. Concealed behind the gold-framed eighteenth-century portrait at left is the door to the kitchen.

"Instant poetry resides in cleverly understated wall finishes," says Deniot of his dining room decor. Custom wallpaper with the subdued gleam of gold threads and crystallized silver is by Callidus Guild, Brooklyn, N.Y., through Jean de Merry showrooms. A framed painting is by Konstantin Kakanias, Los Angeles. The 1840s neo-Roman bronze chandelier is from Gallery Fabien Barbera.

A 1970s wall light by Willy Daro is from Craig Van Den Brulle, New York. The original 1950s set of chairs was designed by Jacques Adnet for UNESCO, Paris, and the 1940s table by Roger Thibier is from Régis Royant gallery. The custom-made Nepalese rug designed by Deniot is a play on marble patterns and was inspired by both ancient Roman marble and Ettore Sottsass' 1980s playful Memphis group faux granite and marble patterns.

For Deniot, the dining table tableau portrays his passion for design exploration, the importance of craft, and purity of line. Swedish 1960s candlesticks are by Gustav Anderson for Ystad Metall. The Louis XVI–period plaster urn is from France.

Creating his very Parisian-chic living room, Deniot relied on unique finds to add the snap and crackle of modernity to the scheme. He also layered each room with wood, faux finishes, bronze, velvet, parchment, wool, metal, alpaca, and linen to give a richly layered effect. A pair of side tables by Paul T. Frankl in parchment, found at an antiques gallery in West Hollywood, support two attenuated 1960s lamps from a consignment store in Los Angeles. The lamps were recolored and given new finishes, but they retained their moonglow/space-age eccentricity. Custom lampshades are by Anne Sokolsky.

Previous pages: Deniot likes a little subversiveness in his own interiors. The large photograph, *Fondation* by Eric Baudelaire, was found at Art Basel, Miami, in 2008. It is a dystopian vision of a wasteland but it gives a lyrical impression. To soften the coved edges of the room, the walls and ceiling were painted in a froth of clouds by Mathias Kiss. The "Waterdrop" bronze coffee table is by Ado Chale from Galerie Yves Gastou. On the table is a massive rock crystal ashtray, a 1930s Macassar ebony cigar box, and a ceramic vase from Hermès.

The 1960s Knoll sofas were purchased in Berlin and covered in "Deluxe" by Zimmer + Rohde. Deniot designed the low-profile lacquered shelves and polished bronze partition dividers in a cubist manner, with a Turkish gray marble mantel. The eighteenth-century plaster bas-relief, "Victory," is from a Roman fragment. The ceramic sculpture is by Pamela Sunday, and the 1930s cubist lamp is from Galerie Teo Leo, Paris. Danish candlesticks on the Turkish marble mantelpiece are by Bjorn Wiinblad in gilt brass and glass, from On Site Antiques, Paris.

The 1796 Directoire period armchair was covered in "Harlequin" tweed. The rug woven by accomplished Nepalese craftsmen was custom designed by Deniot and manufactured by Galerie Diurne. To give the floor an updated antique look, oak planks in different widths were stained in camel/gray with a clear wax polish.

In Deniot's hands, gray is soothing and timeless. Bedroom walls were covered in custom woven striped panels by Georges Le Manach, "Toile de Tour Nacré." The Curtis Jere wall sculpture was crafted in Los Angeles and purchased at a Tajan auction. The tweed headboard was designed by Deniot and covered in "Oscar" by Boussac. The long decorative pillow is by Osborne and Little, and the zebra silk velvet pillow is from Georges Le Manach (recently acquired by Pierre Frey).

Deniot prefers to keep his bed low-key and elegantly simple, with a luxuriously soft spread and throw in handwoven baby alpaca from Alta Pampa. The alcove was upholstered in velvet from Zimmer + Rohde. Ustinov hanging lamps are suspended by a custom-designed bronze bracket. "Hanging lights keep a room uncluttered," notes Deniot. The suede and bronze "Allure" nightstands were designed by Jean-Louis Deniot for his Collection Pierre line. The silk carpet is from Codimat, Paris.

In the dressing room, a dramatic bronze patina sculpture, "Holtevorman," is by Edam H.M.T op ten Berg, Netherlands. Above it hovers a 1960s Curtis Jere chandelier found by Deniot in Los Angeles. Sheer curtains are "Nimbus-Linen" by Sanderson. All storage is concealed behind cabinets with doors of back-painted glass in an abstract onyx pattern. "Cabinets and storage do not have to be wood, or solely functional," says Deniot. "These *verre églomisé* doors reflect light and have a poetic dimension that changes from day to night. In an apartment that is rather subdued, they feel quite rich."

Opposite: Back-painted glass in an abstract onyx pattern was installed on cabinetry. The custom striated bronze door backplate and handle were designed by Deniot.

Antiques galleries in this poetic quartier and on nearby quai Voltaire gleam with gilded furniture and fancy porcelains, tapestries, and precious antiquities.

For Deniot, the location was compelling, but the apartment's large windows, harmonious proportions, and resolutely private feeling were key to this recent acquisition. It's also a three-minute commute to his design studio, an attractive early-morning perk.

"The apartment was very neglected and needed a lot of work, but that meant that I could tailor it very specifically to my own requirements," he recalls. After more than a year of construction and dust, not a millimeter went untouched. Finally the site was transformed into rooms of transcendent beauty, and the superbly modulated interiors paint a subtle portrait of Deniot, his travels, his worldly interests, and his strong belief that even a classical apartment must have a sense of today's directions and desires.

In the master bath, the built-in medicine cabinet was concealed behind a Deniot-designed antiqued silver frame. Small space, dramatic solution: the fluted/striped painted custom-made cabinets match the plaster fluted walls and coved ceilings. The sink is by Duravit, and faucets are by Dornbracht. Nineteenth-century marble urns were purchased in Rome. Flooring is large-slab limestone, and the 1965 chandelier is from On Site Antiques. Agostini sconces in bronze and crystal are from Gallery 88, London.

In the guest bathroom, French limestone and Portuguese Cascais stone were cut into 8.7-centemeter-wide stripes in the style of French artist Daniel Buren. The tub is by Duravit, and fittings are by Dornbracht. The 1950s Danish backlit mirror frame is from On Site Antiques, and the bronze Louis XVI wall lights were purchased from Marc Philippe, Paris.

Previous pages: In the study, which doubles as a self-contained guest suite, walls are decorated with a distinctive custom-designed laser print (with bark inspiration) on linen canvas, designed by Deniot. The corner oak side table is from On Site Antiques. The lamp by Paul Evans, purchased in New York, has a custom lampshade by Anne Sokolsky. The "Loulou" sofa designed by Deniot for his George Smith Collection is covered in "Athina Stripe" by Mulberry Home. The decorative pillow in "Orocolato" is by Dedar. The French 1720 candlesticks in bronze were purchased at an Artcurial auction.

The 1940s André Arbus chair is covered in "Cloud 1" by Kirk Brummel. An early-eighteenth-century family portrait was given to the designer by his grandmother. On the walls, to give a sense of architecture, the brushed oak panels were stained in camel/gray to match the flooring. The 1950s oak and parchment desk by Jacques Adnet was purchased at a Christie's auction. The lamp by Curtis Jere in painted ivory over brass was found in a Los Angeles flea market. The bust is from On Site Antiques. The custom wool rug was designed by Deniot and handcrafted in Nepal for Galerie Diurne. The 1955 Gio Ponti chair was purchased in Milan, and distressed velvet curtains are by Brochier Tradizione.

For all of his custom design projects, Deniot has always chosen to work with exceptionally talented, passionate, and often rather poetic people in Paris, India, Los Angeles, Morocco, and beyond. For the carpets in his apartment he worked closely with Paris-based Galerie Diurne, a custom-carpet company whose founder, Marcel Zelmanovitch, had a Stéphane Mallarmé symbolist poem in mind when he opened the gallery in Saint-Germain-des-Prés in 1982. The classic poem Zelmanovitch had in mind was "Le vierge, le vivace et le bel aujourd'hui" (the incantatory words translate to "The virginal, vivid, and beautiful to-day"). For Zelmanovitch, the poem's first lines inspired his concept that a celebration of the now and present, passion and energy was essential to his new enterprise. "I wanted to bring back to light the great craftsmanship threatened by mass production. My approach is to manufacture one-of-a-kind objects of lasting beauty." From his earliest days, Deniot has made it a practice, a fervent belief, to ally himself with galleries, craftspeople, workshops, design firms, artists, and creators who hold fast to a belief in originality, craft, the symbolic importance of the touch of the hand, as well as aspirations to quality and spirit. In the carpets of his apartment, Deniot continues this tradition.

The kitchen, shimmering and light-filled, is a dream in Paris, where apartment kitchens tend to be tiny and not at all glamorous. The Stilnovo brass and opaline chandelier was purchased from Alexandre Goult gallery. The pair of 1970s Ettore Sottsass ceramic candlesticks is from Galerie Yves Gastou. Fixtures are by Dornbracht. The custom-made cabinets were designed by Deniot, with doors clad in hammered silver and custom-designed matching handles. Countertops are in Carrara marble, and the backsplash is Statuario marble.

FRENCH TRANSLATION,
WITH LAYERS OF NARRATIVE

In the fabled sixth arrondissement, across the river from the Louvre and in the heart of intellectual Paris, stands a sequestered and elegant apartment in a notable eighteenth-century building.

A glimpse of its understated stone exterior, beautifully proportioned and encircled with a lavish twenty-one windows on three sides, suggests that this beauty was untouched since it was first constructed. But Paris real estate is seldom a simple story.

Until just a few years ago the interior of the house was a charmless maze of small, chopped-up rooms. The soaring ceilings, now so soul-stirring, had enticed the previous owners to double the "real estate" by foisting ungainly mezzanines into the grand spaces with an awkward split-level effect.

In the enlarged entry, a quartet of 1850s period prints representing King Louis Philippe's wife, Princess Maria Amalia of Naples and Sicily, and their daughter, Louise d'Orléans, was given graphic black and gold frames and hung in a measured procession of figures and forms. A pair of 1940s Louis XVI–style chairs in ivory patina from Philippe Colangelo, Paris, is covered with black embossed leather.

Alabaster pendants are from Vaughan, London. A bust representing the Ares Borghese was crafted in glazed plaster to resemble ancient dark bronze, by Atelier Prométhée, France. In the hallway, 1810 Empire mahogany armchairs from Jean-François de Blanchetti, Paris, are covered in distressed leather. On the floor, octagonal French limestone has Nero marquina cabochons, installed by Jean-Louis Deniot. Rare French eighteenth-century prints of period hairstyles and hat fashions are from Donald A. Heald, New York. A neoclassical Roman bust will give a room both a note of austere classicism and alluring grandeur, says Deniot.

The 1850s Paris Beaux Arts Roman-style plaster urn is from Fabien Barbera, Paris, mounted as a large lamp by Jean-Louis Deniot. Antique eighteenth-century Italian distressed bronze embroidered fabric was used for a decorative pillow. On the table is a Pierre Frey fabric cloth with silk velvet ribbon and a collection of nineteenth-century neoclassical urns. Deniot transformed an assemblage of antique elements, curtain trimmings, and antique pillows into a unifying dialogue between old and new.

Opposite: An English nineteenth-century rosewood pedestal bar with black marble top is from Drouot auction house, Paris. The decorative pillow is in "Toile de Tours" by Georges Le Manach with a distressed gold ribbon appliqué. The 1940s French Maison Carlhian armchairs have a large middle strip in "Sarona Charcoal" linen on "Sarona Hemp" linen, both from Romo, with the upholstery designed by Deniot.

Previous pages: In the light-filled living room, lined and interlined chocolate brown silk taffeta curtains have a custom embroidered and painted border by Jean-François Lesage. The Roman shades in "Voyage Stripe" are by Jim Thompson. Overhead, the nineteenth-century Italian eighteen-branch, crystal-cut glass chandelier, electrified by Jean-Louis Deniot with tall candle lights, has custom-made lampshades by Anne Sokolsky, Paris. The shape of the custom-designed bronze and glass coffee table by Jean-Louis Deniot in a Brutalist style was dictated by the medallion center of the nineteenth-century French petit point rug from Beauvais Carpets, New York.

The Louis XVI–period gilded sofa from Galerie Ratton Ladrière, Quai Voltaire, Paris, is covered in mohair velvet by Nya Nordiska. The large distressed mirror designed by Jean-Louis Deniot brings a sharper, simpler look to play down the ornaments of the room. A nineteenth-century white marble Venus de Milo sculpture is from Matthieu Monluc, Paris. The French Régence marble fireplace gives the room a sense of authenticity. As part of a program of subtle updates made to the apartment, built-in invisible speakers were mounted in each of the lower rectangles on either side of the fireplace.

Fortunately, a well-traveled American couple acquired it—and through friends discovered Jean-Louis Deniot. Thanks to Deniot, the residence is once again one of the most beautiful in the Faubourg Saint-Germain, with the alluring eighteen-foot-high ceilings restored and the wraparound windows now double-glazed and capturing light. Its comfort and discretion—in a neighborhood that breathes Voltaire's maxim, "A private life is a happy life"—is once more assured.

Deniot was originally signed simply to remodel and reshape the L-shaped floor plan and its confusion of rooms. But he wanted maximum effect, with a smooth enfilade of rooms, a larger entry, graphic plasterwork, antique marble fireplaces, and satin-finished parquet floors.

"It was a handsome Louis XVI-period building, built in the 1870s, with beautifully appointed stonework, arches, and arcades, but these mansions were often built and renovated through the years at top speed and now lacked authentic or top-quality appointments," says Deniot. "In this case, the second floor rooms had been squeezed in with little attention to floor levels. Spiral staircases that had been improvised to reach the upstairs were removed. I also added modern systems, including air conditioning—rare in this historic neighborhood—and concealed sound and security systems."

Deniot loves this Left Bank location, which offers a style compass of Paris and quick access in all directions to dining, fashion, culture, art, and music. And his clients, he says, are very much at home in Paris. They were active participants in the design process of their residence. In Paris and New York they acquired a richly detailed Bessarabian carpet and a beguiling collection of gold-framed portraits of colorfully dressed courtiers, kings, queens, and nobles.

Chandeliers sparkle and bring a lighthearted mood, colors are subtle, silks shimmer, and muscular silhouettes of sofas and chairs give the rooms an elegant delineation and crisp perfection. It's a French design story with a happy ending: a dream realized for a fortunate couple.

The Directoire-period mahogany trumeau above the library fireplace is from Galerie François Belliard, Paris. The 1880s black ebony bench is from Bruno Le Yaouanc, Marché Paul Bert, Paris. A pair of 1940s Maison Carlhian settees is from Galerie Edouard de la Marque, Paris. The custom-made dark bronze reading lamps are by Jean-Louis Deniot. Vertical elements echo and emphasize the high-ceilinged room.

Previous pages: New door pediments designed by Jean-Louis Deniot emphasize the ceiling height of the library. The forged iron, distressed gold-leaf finish, and Macassar ebony bookcases were designed by Deniot. The 1940 Maison Carlhian sofa was covered in Pierre Frey velvet. The custom rug is by Gallery Diurne. Faux painted double doors make a fresh and subtle textural addition.

Also in the library design, a nineteenth-century French pedestal table, an Empire mahogany desk, a Directoire-period mahogany chair, and 1880 neoclassical bronze lamps present a cohesive roomscape. To add structure to the window treatments, Deniot applied ribbon trim to the silk roman shades.

In the master bedroom, a neoclassical plaster statue is reflected in a Louis XVI–period trumeau mirror. The wall-mounted lights are from Maison Jansen.

Opposite: The 1820 Italian gilt wood and crystal glass bead chandelier is from Galerie Vonthron, Paris. Graceful and subtle, the canopy bed decor was designed by Jean-Louis Deniot in "Les Perles" from Georges Le Manach, with silk lining from Dedar. The baby alpaca bed throw from Alta Pampa offers simple luxury. In contrast is an elaborate Louis XV gilt wood "Rocaille" bench from François Belliard Antiques, Paris, covered in "Highlands Avonio" by Rubelli. A poetic chandelier in a high-ceilinged bedroom provides an idyllic focal point from the bed.

In the charming guest suite are a Louis XVI–period mirror and chest. The hand-printed cotton for the wall up-holstery is from India. A busy wall motif in a small bedroom will divert attention from the room's petite size, says Deniot. Similarly, a somewhat large bed gives a small room a bold sense of importance.

Bedroom decor includes striped fabric by Pierre Frey, custom-designed reading lamps by Deniot, and decorative pillows in "Coppelia-Percale" by Edmond Petit, originally designed by Madeleine Castaing. The custom-made, hand-stitched baby alpaca bedspread and throw are by Alta Pampa. Deniot notes that a beautifully draped canopy brings chic and drama to a small bedroom.

Previous pages: In the wife's bathroom, lanterns are by Vaughan, London. The elegant eighteenth-century plaster urns are from Julien Régnier, Paris. The custom-framed butterfly collection is from Deyrolle, Paris. French limestone and Carrara checkboard flooring was designed by Deniot. "To prevent a bathroom from feeling too cold, use roman shades and drapes," he says.

Fittings from Volevatch are in polished nickel. Traditional and voluptuous, the bathtub by Jacob Delafon is in enameled steel. Cabinetry, a wooden painted surround, and room paneling were designed by Deniot, who matched the bathroom color palette and decor to the bedroom's heightened sense of personal space.

IN THE REALM OF THE INTELLECT

Boulevard Saint-Germain is a dream of broad sidewalks for meandering, despite traffic flying helter-skelter. There are neighborhood seductions and diversions: antiques galleries, bookshops, art galleries, and Romanesque churches to explore. Punctuating the panorama are tall, arched doorways and centuries-old stone walls. Occasionally, a massive dark-green lacquered door will open a few inches, offering a glimpse of a cobblestone courtyard, a portico to a hidden apartment, and other private worlds of French style.

It is in just such a discreet location, on the top floor of a corner building overlooking the sycamores, that a French family acquired a two-level apartment, with views of the Hôtel des Invalides and the Eiffel Tower in the distance. From the main floor, a staircase leads up to a guest suite and studio. Light spills in from all directions, giving a sense of floating on Parisian air.

In the entry hall, above, the curved wall of cabinets follows the line of the stairway and landing. Strips of bleached oak streak across gray-painted cabinet doors, concealing secret storage. A pair of 1970s black leather chairs is by Oscar Tusquets, Spain. The 1970 Lucite easel is attributed to American designer Charles Hollis Jones. Overhead, custom-made lanterns with a distressed gold-leaf lining are by Deniot, who emphasized the room's curved shape using sinuous wall details and custom rugs. "Don't fight it: rather, work with it," he says. The curved carpet was designed by Deniot for Galerie Diurne, with an off-kilter Greek key border pattern, inspired by concepts sketched by the Parisian artist Christian Bérard.

Opposite: In the dining room, a set of ten Louis XVI–style dining chairs is upholstered in Zimmer + Rohde "Prion" and Boussac "Sirocco." Deniot likes to use one fabric on the seat and another on the back, for individuality and to modulate the repetition. The vase on a Lucite stand is by Gaetano Pesce. The bronze and dark oak dining table was designed by Deniot. Oak wall panels slide to conceal china storage. The 1950s armchair by Jansen is upholstered in Pierre Frey tailoring-inspired twill and the 1950s chandelier is by Stilnovo.

"Well, the apartment wasn't exactly charming when we first inspected it," notes Jean-Louis Deniot. It was built in the 1870s Haussmann style, with all of the attendant installed-by-the-numbers, mass-produced fireplaces and sentimental attempts at Louis-the-Something plasterwork. The floor plan was also problematic, with awkward transitions and a lack of logic. "My clients are very worldly and have great style, so they knew the overdone crown moldings with plaster angels and acanthus leaves would have to go," notes the designer.

"For this new pied-à-terre I kept only the classical paneled doors and cleared out the rest. I demolished it because the installations of the late 1800s were very heavy-handed. Haussmann was inventing Paris, and it had to be done fast. It was of-the-period Napoleon III styles and Empire mixed together, and all in the wrong proportions. There was no question: we were starting from scratch."

A 1950s red cap lamp attributed to Louis Kalf was purchased in Los Angeles, where Deniot keeps a residence, the better to scoop up rare vintage trophies. The carpet by Galerie Diurne was designed by Deniot. The 1950s Maison Jansen chromed metal fireplace gives a flash of modernity in the scheme. The crisp etched mirror and fireplace surround were designed by Deniot. The versatile floor lamp table is attributed to Jaques Adnet. Paintings are by Jean-Michel Atlan. Deniot notes that a demi-lune, wedge, or oddly shaped room is best highlighted using custom-manufactured furniture. Here the bookcases expertly accentuate the wall's curve.

Previous pages: The apartment is shaped like a yacht, so Deniot outfitted it like a luxury vessel, with very precise cabinetry, custom-designed seating, efficient storage, and a "porthole" built into the bookcase. The curved sofa in the living room was custom crafted by Collection Pierre and upholstered in Zimmer + Rhode's "Paso." The large 1950s free-form coffee table by T. H. Robsjohn-Gibbings was found in Los Angeles. The fitted quarter-moon carpet by Galerie Diurne was made by skilled craftsmen in Nepal.

The Bertoia bar chairs are by Knoll. Deniot created a custom kitchen composition, mixing horizontal and vertical oak grain cabinet surfaces with stainless steel accents. He designed a *dégradé* frosted glass and steel screen to provide separation between rooms.

Deniot plans for function both within the room and in repose on the bed. The two night-stands are "Insomnie N° 333" by Hervé Van der Straeten, with a pair of 1950s Danish porcelain lamps. Unobtrusive, independently operated, articulated lights make reading in bed very comfortable. Deniot places them in every bedroom. The bed is framed with, in effect, a pair of headboards to soften sound and add stature to an understated sequence of furnishings. The larger headboard is framed with brushed oak that matches the room's doorframes. The armchair by Deniot for Collection Pierre is upholstered with John Hutton fabric, "Moody Blues." A small guéridon with a gold-leaf base and fossil top by Philippe Hiquily is from Galerie Yves Gastou. The decorative wall upholstery is in Dominique Kieffer's "Glacé Gris Clair."

Two sheer horsehair roman blinds are in Le Crin "Pegase." The pair of cast-iron lamps, Clignancourt trove, is in the style of Giacometti. The cabinet in brushed walnut by Gio Ponti is from Galerie Régis Royant.

In the attic studio/bedroom suite, the 1950s armchair and 1960s lamp were treasures from the weekend Fairfax flea market in Los Angeles. The view, which glances over the venerable rooftops of Saint-Germain, includes the gilded dome of Les Invalides (the tomb of Napoleon) and the Eiffel Tower, which is particularly entertaining at night when, on the hour, a psychedelic light show is illuminated.

The corner daybed designed by Deniot is upholstered in mohair velvet from Kirk Brummel. The 1950s decoupage Italian lamp is in the style of Fornasetti. Ceramics are from On Site Antiques.

Deniot introduced a sleek version of classic Left Bank Bohemian history. He looked to Man Ray and Constructivist art, and proposed the idea of an arty mix of gold-framed paintings from the school of Rubens, as well as flea market finds and contemporary artist-designed furniture.

"The floor plan was originally completely asymmetrical, so I decided to play with that, not fight it," says Deniot. "I emphasized the half-moon shape of the living room with a fitted bookcase, then brought in a low-key 'Kiki de Montparnasse'-style glass and iron partition between the kitchen and family room." Today the apartment is the perfect Parisian refuge: fresh, relaxed, and architecturally perfect. It is equidistant between the Café de Flore and Barthélemy, the best cheese shop in Paris, and a brisk walk from Deniot's studio.

In the guest suite, the storage chest at the end of the bed is upholstered in "Grégoire" and an armchair is upholstered in "Charade," both by Kirk Brummel. The simple bedspread is in Nya Nordiska "Kakuki." In the stairway, above, the "Origami" mirror by Pouenat was custom finished for Deniot, who likes to combine functionality, art, and practicality. Here the wall sculpture is both a mirror and a wall light.

HISTORIC DOMAIN, MODERN SPIRIT

Jean-Louis Deniot's cohesive and understated approach to renewing the grand traditions of French interior design and architecture is evident in every corner of a private apartment he completed in a highly desirable Left Bank *quartier*.

Light-filled rooms enjoy all the hallmarks of classical French residential structures, with high ceilings and beautiful proportions. An airy enfilade of large door openings gives the appearance of a much larger space. But for all the elegance, the apartment feels modern, light, and fresh, with contemporary furniture, graphic collections of art, sculptures by Hervé Van der Straeten, eccentric antiques, and simple but luxurious fabrics like sleek mohair, baby alpaca, and silk velvet.

In the entry, Deniot placed a mirror at one end to create the illusion of an enfilade and to give the "pass-through" area a feeling of welcome and magic. A pair of lanterns by Gilbert Poillerat is light and sculptural.

Armchairs by Jean-Charles Moreux with new appliqué embellishment give a sense of gravitas. And there's a custom-made console embroidered by Jean-François Lesage that is both decorative and practical, providing storage for umbrellas, rainboots, and toy yachts to sail on the pond in the Jardin du Luxembourg. The studded mirror with antiqued glass was designed by Deniot, who believes that a mirror mosaic on a large wall in lieu of a single piece will guarantee a mysterious effect with no harsh reflection.

A pair of 1970 lamps is from Maison Charles. The large 1940 neoclassical plaster vase suggests Jean-Michel Frank. The floor is salvaged eighteenth-century French stone to suggest that it is original to the building.

Deniot's overarching concept was to make the apartment look as if it had come together over centuries, not months. He avoids an all-new style, mixing new custom pieces (beds, sofas, dining chairs) with serendipitous vintage and antique accents. The mix: a custom-made sofa by Collection Pierre and embroidered by Jean-François Lesage, with time-honored one-of-a-kind designs by some of the great Paris furniture designers. The coffee table by André Arbus displays the designer's classical architectural lines and craftsmanship. End tables are by Charles Moreux.

In counterpoint to the foliate pattern on the plaster walls, Deniot selected a pair of lamps with a crisp silhouette by André Arbus, purchased from Galerie Yves Gastou. The alabaster sconces by Pouenat and the X-stools by Raymond Subes present 1930s lineage to the room. The custom-woven wool carpet is by Galerie Diurne. Custom plaster walls are by Deniot. The large-scale painting is an introspective self-portrait by the contemporary Scottish figurative painter Stephen Conroy.

Above: The custom-made sofa by Collection Pierre is embellished with hand-stitched quilting. The pillows were embroidered with a motif after a Gilbert Poillerat mirror design, by Jean-François Lesage. The alabasters are vintage.

Deniot chose round tables by Collection Pierre for versatility: they can be used for a romantic breakfast à deux, an informal lunch, a brief afternoon tea, cocktail hour, or a more formal dinner with friends. Smaller round tables don't convey the massive presence of one very large dining table in a room. Dining chairs are by Royère. The room's gold-leaf-on-steel sconces are by Hervé Van der Straeten. "The black painted dining tabletop reflects and mirrors the festive Murano chandelier overhead and introduces a captivating element to the room," says Deniot.

In the alcove, above, silk velvet seating adds a luxurious theatricality. Pillows are by Jean-François Lesage. The floor lamps, with petite attached cocktail/candle trays, were designed by Deniot. Meticulously lined Roman shades were crafted in Jagtar silk. Deniot improvised traditional mattress seating and simple pillows covered in elegant silk velvet for a superb custom-looking sofa.

Previous pages: The green/gray mohair-covered 1940s armchairs are by Jacques Adnet. The grand lacquered buffet, a classic choice for Paris apartments, is by Gilbert Poillerat, from Galerie Yves Gastou. A pair of lamps by André Arbus on the buffet is also from Yves Gastou. The plaster chandelier in the style of Giacometti, designed by Deniot, is intended to animate the room and offer airy gestural shapes overhead. The bronze-frame mirror was designed by Jean-Louis Deniot.

The kitchen was given a chic breakfast-room feeling with diamond-shape bleached light oak built-in cabinetry. A light fixture/hanging rack and chairs designed by Deniot are all in bleached oak and blackened bronze. The 1950s sconces are from Régis Royant. The dining room and adjacent kitchen were given similar tones and materials so the transition is not abrupt. The area rug is by Galerie Diurne, and the bronze and parchment bookshelf was designed by Jean-Louis Deniot.

In the bedroom, the gilded forged-iron lamps on the antique marble fireplace mantel are by Gilbert Poillerat. The small 1940s André Arbus mirror is placed in front of the grand gilded Louis XVI–period mirror to break up the expanse of reflection, a deft Deniot device.

The bedroom decor was planned around perfect light control (the airy silk curtains are lined and interlined as intricately as a couture jacket) and the comfort needed for a long-distance traveler. (The couple flies in from New York or Aspen.) Deniot always makes a point of providing independently controlled lights at each side of the bed, with overhead reading lights as well. The almost kinetic sculptural mirror above the bed is by Hervé Van der Straeten. A pair of custom shagreen nightstands by R. & Y. Augousti is accompanied by a pair of 1940s lamps by Serge Roche.

The bed is by Collection Pierre, and the area rug is by Galerie Diurne. In the foreground is a gestural 1940s Roger Thibier table. Silk pillows are by Jim Thompson. Sconces were custom designed by Jean-Louis Deniot. The bedcover is designed with handwoven baby alpaca from the Argentinean company Alta Pampa. Deniot applied simple bands of grosgrain ribbon to a painted wall for an elegant paneling effect.

Deniot's response to designing a small bathroom: "I drew inspiration from a ballroom to design a bathroom! It's small but glamorous, especially the crystal sconces and shimmering lighting. Bold experimentation in decorating a rather small dimension can make a sizeable difference and a great impact," he says.

The bathroom is lavished with mirrors to give the appearance of endless space. Deniot deployed one of his classic design methods to prevent the expanses of mirror from seeming too "new": above the bath, the mirror is in mosaic sections that break up the expanse and give the effect of glitter.

Wall lights are by Maison Baguès, and a 1940s crystal chandelier is by Serge Roche. The custom-designed countertop is honed Bardiglio Turquin marble, an elegant stone from an Italian quarry with a signature blue tone and dove gray striations. It stands on a custom vanity in a 1940 chest of drawers design with antiqued mirror.

PETIT PIED-À-TERRE

Located in one of the most historic and atmospheric *quartiers* of the Left Bank, quiet rue Jacques Callot is lined by art galleries. The adjoining rue de Seine is cheek-to-cheek with all the best dealers in twentieth-century antiques (think Jean Dunand, Pierre Chareau, and Jacques-Émile Ruhlmann). Through a hidden door, and up four twisting flights of stairs with the heady fragrance of old wood and beeswax, is this petite suite, with a living room/dining room, a sunny bedroom, secret closets to hide computers, wine bottle storage, and a meticulous dressing room.

Deniot's design art and sleight-of-hand make this jewel-box apartment feel spacious. He played with scale to great effect. Grand mirrors, bold and sculptural furnishings, and vivid large-scale collections with jolts of color transformed this tiny Paris treasure into an endlessly fascinating retreat.

Jean-Louis Deniot feels that a dynamic and graphic rug enhances a room's visual energy. He deployed a bold striped carpet, inspired by the sharp, tart colors used with great panache by designer Madeleine Castaing, whose trend-setting shop on rue Jacob was once just a five-minute walk away. To give the room architecture and focus, Deniot designed a fireplace in limestone. The 1940s marble table was discovered at the Marché Paul Bert at Clignancourt. The ceramic bowl is by Marianne Vissière, and the plaster urn lamp from the Paris flea market has a shade by Anne Sokolsky. Deniot believes in the bold, confident placement of large mirrors, new and antique. He found the rosewood mirror, circa 1850, at Marché Serpette. Serge Roche plaster lights line the walls.

The armchairs designed by Deniot are covered in a practical ponyskin. Dark chocolate brown is a unifying theme throughout the apartment—used dramatically on frames, doors, lampshades, and upholstery. The niche was created (and emphasized with gray-green wall fabric) to add a visual exclamation point. It creates the sense of a separate space for quiet reading and relaxation. A framed portrait, circa 1840, is in the style of Rembrandt. The sofa is Louis XVI style, and light fixtures are from Van Baggum Collecties, The Netherlands. The ivory-colored wall is painted in trompe-l'oeil patterns to resemble parchment. Deniot notes, "The faux parchment wall finish contributes both a rich textural background and a sense of refined architecture to a room."

Deniot designed closets to hide mundane essential household equipment, keeping main spaces clean and attractive. He believes in using furniture that is somewhat large in scale in small rooms—to give a sense of importance and definition as well as for pure comfort. Deniot says, "Overscale elements fool the eye and contribute to expanding a space."

The gilt sunburst (working) clock above the bed is 1940s, by Maison Jansen. "A strong striped motif above the headboard makes a dramatic statement and is all the more fitting as it cannot be seen from the bed," notes Deniot. The wardrobe and dressing rooms are disguised behind doors to the right and left of the bed. "Never hesitate to sacrifice a minimum of living space to accommodate a maximum of closet space," says Deniot. Pillows are in silk/cotton by Jim Thompson, and gold brass wall lamps are by Maison Jansen. On the console is a 1930s plaster bust. The plaster bas relief is also from the 1930s. The 1985 black and white photos are by Karl Lagerfeld.

SPLENDOR OVERLOOKING THE SEINE

Perfectly poised on Ile St. Louis in the heart of Paris, this building is in one of the loveliest and quietest locations in Paris. Facades of discreet classical limestone residences turn toward the early morning light, and in the afternoon, the churning wake of pleasure boats sends sunrays magically flickering through apartment windows and across ceilings and walls.

It is here, along a cobblestone street, that Jean-Louis Deniot recently designed an ultraprivate retreat for a California family involved in the worlds of new technology. From their bedroom windows, the flying buttresses of Notre-Dame loom to the west, and in the evening, restaurants of the Left Bank are just a quick walk away.

In the high-ceilinged entry, Deniot covered the walls with two-foot-by-two-foot panels of parchment, an elegant and practical wall covering. "It's very pale and ivory, not yellow," he notes. To give the concept more power, he had the crown molding and baseboards painted with a faux parchment effect.

Grace notes for the entry decor include a 1940s Venetian mirror from Galerie Jacques Lafon. The 1940s wall console by Ramsey is like a quick sketch, light and useful, without taking any floor space. The wool rug is by Galerie Diurne, and the 1950s coat stand is by Roger Ferrand. The new hand railing was designed by Deniot with clean neoclassical lines. On the marble-topped console, the Gio Ponti ceramic is from Galerie Yves Gastou. The bronze Roman emperor bust sculpture, which offers a certain gravitas, is from Galerie Bazin, Paris. Reflected in the mirror is the adjacent living room.

The family residence, originally built in the late seventeenth century, is hidden behind a massive portal that leads from the street into a discreet courtyard and portico.

The original concept for updating the two-story residence was simply to improve the floor plan, which was somewhat cramped. But for Jean-Louis Deniot, always a perfectionist, it was essential to make fundamental interior architecture corrections to his client's new acquisition, and to erase years of ill-informed changes so that the five-bedroom apartment would reach its potential.

"It's an elegant building, with a grand stone staircase that leads up to the apartment entry and tall windows to capture quintessential Paris views. The building is strong and pure, with great architectural integrity, but this apartment had been chopped up into a series of small rooms," notes Deniot. "It was originally home to courtiers of the king, to bankers and nobles."

Deniot loves a mix—of periods, artists, metals, and points of view. The large Louis XV gilt corbeille sofa is from Auction Drouot. The 1940 desk from Maison Jansen, from On Site Antiques, has a Hiquily swan lamp from Galerie Yves Gastou. The Hiquily console with onyx top is also from Yves Gastou. A comfortable 1940s armchair by André Arbus is covered in Westbury fabric. The custom rug is by Galerie Diurne. A bronze and rock chandelier is by Hervé Van der Straeten. The graphic artwork is Ruth Francken's *La Manif*. Deniot likes the vibrant and vivid effect of juxtaposition and variety in his designs. Each piece has its own character and is shown to advantage jostling with contrasting works.

Following pages: An abstract bronze sculpture is signed Tao Sigulda. The Ruth Francken *Portrait of Iannis Xenakis* is from Galerie Yves Gastou. The 1950s abstract feminine sculptural wood lamp, signed Marianna Von Allesch, is from On Site Antiques, as is the Harry Bertoia "Sputnik" sculpture. Bold and graphic, the one-of-a-kind console by McCollin Bryan, London, makes a fine placement for the large neoclassical alabaster urn lamp from Galerie Edouard de La Marque. A pair of marble obelisks is from On Site Antiques.

"The entry stairs were made very wide so that two ladies in crinoline could walk side by side. So I wanted to re-create beautifully proportioned new interiors, bring back the high level of craftsmanship, and maximize my client's property."

Deniot arranged an inspection and study of the apartment with the new owners. "It was disappointing to see how much this historic apartment had been ruined. My first impulse was not to start simple cosmetic changes but to bring in the bulldozer. The structure required major work. After discussions with my client, we decided to proceed with detailed engineering studies. Then, very well-informed, we were able to plan much more extensive improvements."

The window in the bedroom, so crucial for light and views, had earlier been boarded up because an admired French president did not want the residents of this apartment overlooking his own residence. Deniot was determined to have it returned—and succeeded. The green curtains are Veraseta iridescent silk, carefully interlined. The 1940s Louis XV/XVI-transition-style low alcove sofa is by Jansen, covered in Sabina Fay Braxton hand-crafted fabric.

In design detail, framing the precious new view is a shade from Edmond Petit "Starlight." The central zebra pillow is covered in Jim Thompson "Illusion." Side pillows are in Loro Piana cashmere, and the corner pillow is in Holland & Sherry cashmere. Reading lamps are from Galerie des Lampes. The coffee table is by Fernand Dresse, Galerie Yves Gastou, and the custom thousand-stripes carpet is by Galerie Diurne.

Previous pages: Modern, ancient, refined, and raw are all in the fascinating mix. The gold-leaf Louis XVI–style frame has a custom two-way mirror (to hide the TV screen). The Roger Bezombes *medaille L'Enfer* is from Galerie Yves Gastou, as is an André Arbus stone *masque*. To offer a sense of a lifetime of collecting, Deniot chose two sixteenth-century paintings attributed to Jean Cousin and Christian Demenstien.

Excavating the building and taking rooms carefully and respectfully down to the studs was like archaeology, says the designer. "We found old reused ship timbers, and in the living room we discovered hand-printed wallpaper dating back to the eighteenth century. We had great admiration for the life of the apartment, its history. My concept was to return to its neoclassical origins. Over the centuries it had been carelessly altered: a view window was covered up; rooms were sliced and diced. The key was to remove these problems, and bring out its beauty, its grace."

Slowly, alignments were made, as Deniot focused first on the architecture, reworking the walls, opening poorly proportioned doorways, reshaping the floor plan. New systems, including electrical and security, were added in the process, with everything in the right place. Deniot was always alert to the aesthetics—breathtaking enfilades of rooms, perfectly placed fireplaces—and equally to the practical and functional aspects.

On the Louis XVI–style white marble chimneypiece from Galerie Marc Maison are white porcelain *bonbonnières*. Parchment lamps are by Alexandre Biaggi, rue de Seine, Paris.

In the bedroom, all paneling and interior architecture was designed by Deniot. The Jean Roze canopy fabric has Louis XVI–period crowns. The Alta Pampa baby alpaca bedspread has Colefax & Fowler decorative pillows. The Louis XVI–period headboards have their original antique patina. Even with period furnishings, Deniot adds essential adjustable reading lamps. The leather saddle-stitched lamp is by Jacques Adnet, and wall upholstery is in Georges Le Manach fabrics.

His creative empathy is evident now in each room, public and private. The living room, in particular, displays Deniot's visually acute sense of historical French interiors. He had all of the walls paneled by French specialists. The brushed and waxed oak paneling is simply finished, somewhat matt, with the oak grain visible. It feels as if it has softly aged, as if it had been there from the start. New ten-foot-high doors, highly lacquered and shiny, give the room a sense of grandeur and lightness.

"You can also see the grain of the wood, with its waxed patina, in the chunky oak casing around the doors," says Deniot.

The designer notes that in this apartment, as in most of his projects, he treated the crown molding as if it were part of the walls. It curves up the wall and into the ceiling space. "In France, generally, the crown simply matches the paneling, but great British architects like Robert Adam and Charles Cameron saw it as part of the ceiling," he says. "My style of lifting the crown molding up into the perimeter of the ceiling gives the wall added height. It enhances the verticality, reduces a boring ceiling, and gives the room a proper finish. I believe it gives the decor a sense of polish and encloses the people in the room."

The guest bedroom gains glamour and delight from an Empire period *corbeille* (basket) pendant chandelier. Decorative pillows are covered in Lelièvre fabric. The custom-designed headboard by Jean-Louis Deniot is covered in Zimmer + Rohde velvet. Georges Le Manach wall upholstery fabric is custom colored. The new seventeenth-century-inspired bed alcove designed by Jean-Louis Deniot has concealed storage and bed lighting. The Diurne rug is custom made.

In detail, the Veraseta Roman shades have grosgrain ribbon appliqués. The Jim Thompson silk drapes have Dedar "marabou" trim. The dazzling chair is "Ammonite" by Claude de Muzac.

Other rooms were also sympathetically restored, with a light touch. Upstairs, bedrooms now have charm and style, with fresh details, uncomplicated modern comforts.

"This was a wonderful project, and I admire and appreciate my clients so much for seeing it through," says Deniot. "Now guests arrive and comment about how 'well-preserved' the apartment is, under the impression that everything is original. The family is very happy."

The guest bedroom includes a new Empire-style gilt frame with a two-way mirror to hide the TV screen. A gold-leaf high-back Consulate period armchair from Galerie Fabien Barbera is covered in Verel de Belval silk velvet. The straw marquetry sideboard was designed by Jean-Louis Deniot in the iconic Jean-Michel Frank style.

In a bedroom that is all soft surfaces, Deniot likes the surprise of a 1950s decorative ceramic vase from On Site Antiques and the *Clairon* sculpture by Catherine Caba from Galerie Yves Gastou. The black and white photo by Ivan Kafka is a little subdued alongside Hervé Van der Straeten Constructivist-style lamps in parchment and black ebony.

THE INTERPRETATION OF DREAMS

In a chic residential quartier of Paris near the UNESCO headquarters, where tourists seldom venture, stands a 1930s classic limestone apartment building, encircled with balconies. It's the very private world of an influential art collector who moved back to Paris recently as the art scene became more vital. She wanted to be involved with the arts of the city and to follow artists of interest.

The luxurious 2,600-square-foot apartment she acquired had a perfect floor plan, with beautiful all-day light, an enfilade of rooms, and large expanses of walls for her provocative and significant collection of paintings and sculpture. She engaged Jean-Louis Deniot to restructure the apartment layout to fit her specific requirements for both art display and comfortable day-to-day living.

On the terrace stands a 2006 glass sculpture by artist Jean-Michel Othoniel (designer of the glass-jeweled Metro entrance near the Comédie Francaise). "Balconies and other outdoor spaces need thoughtful and interesting ornament, decoration, and art," says Deniot. "This piece changes with the light and is fascinating in all seasons. The perfect choice."

In the apartment office, opposite, a built-in stained oak desk provides a springboard for inspiration. The Napoleon III tufted chair is covered in Brunschwig & Fils satin. The height of Paris buildings is strictly limited, so views like this one of the Eiffel Tower will never be obscured by new construction.

In the entry, art is given prominence. The sculpture is *Edouard* (2006) by Xavier Veilhan. Overhead is the glimmer of a 1960s chandelier by Venini. The stainless steel console was custom made by Hervé Van der Straeten. To provide curves and additional sculpture, Deniot added a pair of 1930s parchment chairs. On the left is a mirror/artwork, *To Be Titled* (2005) by Daniel Buren, a French national treasure who created the abstract series of black and white sculpted columns that surprise visitors to the Palais Royal in Paris.

Opposite: The photograph *Paradise 25* (2011) is by Thomas Struth, who commented on his *Paradise* series taken in China, California, and Australia: "I didn't want to portray a specific place. Rather I was trying to feel within its primeval branchings the moment of beginning that once was the world." The floor stone, lightly patterned, is laid in a subtle abstract pattern.

Following pages: Four pieces of art are by Sophie Calle. The armchairs and day bed are by George Smith, London. The carpet is by Galerie Diurne, Paris. An art piece in its own right, the 1960s glass chandelier is by Venini. The mirror and fireplace designed by Deniot are positioned to be in balance. The shagreen coffee table was designed by Deniot. The piece to the left of the fireplace is *Nude and Cactus* by Antony Williams. In contrast to the curves of the daybed, the Jean-Michel Frank sofa is crisp and tailored.

In the dining room, Deniot took down the color a few notches to make it more atmospheric at night. The 1960s chandelier is by Venini. Chairs are by Collection Pierre. The artwork to the left of the room is *Yellow Hallway #2* (2001) by James Casebere. The carpet by Galerie Diurne, Paris, is in a pale cubist pattern that mimics shadows of furniture across the wool and silk surface. The 2006 sculpture *Xavier (Capuche)* is by Xavier Veilhan, and the large painting, *N.13*, is by Bernard Frize.

Previous pages: Deniot notes that the art-loving homeowner wanted to avoid the look of a gallery or museum, believing that art is part of daily life, merely enhanced by simple lamps so as not to be "arrogantly on display" or "demanding attention." Walls were paneled discreetly and painted in soft, chalky off-white gradations. "Stark white was banished from the apartment," says Deniot. "Art does not look good on bright white. The color here is more like a soft off-white plaster, very soft, not at all cold." The silver side table/stool is by Hervé Van der Straeten. The piece to the left of the room is *Heaven Above/ Hell Below* (2003) by Damien Hirst. The painting on the right of the room is by Pierre Soulages (2004). The painting/wall installation on the far left of the room is by Christian Boltanski.

And there was no question, says Deniot, that the glitzy flashes of gold, the shiny acres of marble, and the formulaic and fussy crown moldings the previous owner favored would disappear. "It's so pleasant up there, with views of the Eiffel Tower that are always exciting, beautiful trees, a discreet sense of privacy, and all-day sun," says Deniot. "We just had to pare it down, get back a little of the art deco style of its early days. I removed all the excess and took it back to basics."

After twelve months of demolition work, the space was completely revised, with all flooring and surfaces changed. "There is not one hint of the previous apartment, as we changed the masonry and added simple new plasterwork, new woodwork, new marble and stone flooring, new decorative painting, mirrors, and glasswork," says Deniot. And there was the obligatory installation of new electrical wiring, a new security and sound/video system, and new heating and plumbing. "The idea was to present the illusion that only the paint had been refreshed—that the apartment had always looked this way, with museum-quality art brought in."

In the bedroom, the colorful cabinet is by artist Mattia Bonetti. The armchairs are by Sean Cooper. The piece over the commode is *Fuck, Fuck, Fuck You* (2005) by Tracy Emin. The headboard is by Collection Pierre.
Opposite: The photograph *Le Lait Miraculeux de la Vierge* (1997) is by Bettina Rheims. The carpet, with neat geometrical patterns, is by David Hicks. Baubles in the ceiling are part of *Les Amants Suspendus* (1999) by Jean-Michel Othoniel.

As the demolition proceeded, Deniot developed a very neutral palette for rooms, with earth tones and barely-there colors like ivory, parchment, and soft white (known in French as *blanc cassé,* or broken white). "It was important to establish harmony and balance among the pieces of art, the furniture, the decor," he says. He used glazes in tobacco tones, along with raffia and wild silk at the base of walls to add depth, texture, and framing to the spaces.

"The owner's art collection is very interesting and current, as she is an avid collector who is intrepid and ironic in her choices. She does not hesitate to buy pieces that others refuse," he says. In the decor, Deniot created a certain formality in juxtaposition with the uncompromising art, while allowing the statements and strengths of each piece to push through. His art-loving client expressed her pleasure, and Deniot has since designed art-filled residences for her in other capitals. Mission accomplished, dream fulfilled.

For the bathroom Deniot selected a Volevatch towel rack. The Cascais stone tiles are from Portugal. Sconces were custom designed by Deniot.

Opposite: The carpet in the guest bedroom is by David Hicks. The coffee table in sycamore and bronze is by Garouste and Bonetti. The bed was custom made by Collection Pierre. The artwork, *Epaule fil d'âne,* is by Gérard Garouste.

TIMELESS PARIS,
SILHOUETTES INTENSIFIED

Fortunate, indeed, are a couple who live in a handsome 1911 apartment Jean-Louis Deniot designed in the shadow of the Eiffel Tower. Situated on a very private, tree-shaded street, the apartment offers up-close views of the intricate tracery of the Meccano-esque obelisk as it zigzags up into the clouds.

At night, a powerful laser light positioned at its three-hundred-meter-high peak circles overhead, mesmerizing and graceful.

"This is one of the most desirable locations in Paris, just near the Champs de Mars, but quite hidden and beautifully secluded," says Deniot, who is always acutely sensitive to the settings of the residences he designs.

"The family wanted very classic interiors, so we chose Directoire style—very strict and a little stiff and formal, but with elegance and softness," says Deniot. There is a lot of detail to the arches and columns. The wallcoverings and paneling were meticulously conceived, and Deniot and his team designed lavish curtains, as well as custom-crafted silk and wool carpets. The upholstery is plush and comfortable. It's the quintessential Paris apartment.

The Eiffel Tower is a comforting presence just across the apartment's garden—a sentinel, in effect. In the living room, the Louis XVI bergères are from Thierry Ferrand, Marché Serpette, in Saint-Ouen. The 1940s Jansen Empire-style side table is in ebony and mahogany. The turn-of-the-century French alabaster lamp has a custom shade by Anne Sokolsky, Paris. The zebra bolster is in "Illusion" from Jim Thompson. "I kept the curtains very simple, with a layer of sheer and then luscious silk," says Deniot. "At night, the family doesn't always close them. On the hour, they love to see the festive lights on the Eiffel Tower flashing." The large 1930s sun clock in gilt wood is from On Site Antiques.

Following pages: The custom-made, hand-painted side table has a skirt by Jean-François Lesage, embroidered with brass and pewter threads. The fringe is made of silk with bells on each tassel. The large-scale photograph is by William Curtis Rolf. Deniot notes that a perfectly circular rug in this pentagonal room harmonizes the off-balance room shape.

A Directoire fireplace is the focal point of the living room. The French 1850 black marble clock is from Galerie Fabien Barbera. Deniot designed the ultra-tall arches that circle the rooms. The wall paneling was given a distressed finish by a specialized painter using traditional French techniques of glazing, trompe l'oeil, and *faux bois* in beige, gray, and ivory. The "Pompeii" sconces are from Galerie des Lampes. The fireplace is double-sided—visible also in the dining room—to widen the fire's reach and render the atmosphere welcoming and convivial.

The couple loves to entertain, so the dining room takes pride of place, with a nineteenth-century mahogany table from Matthieu Monluc, Paris, and a set of six chairs and two armchairs, Louis XVI style, from Fabien Barbera, Paris. The large French 1940 Baguès chandelier is from Galerie William Vonthron, Paris. The 1820 mahogany console has a black marble top. The large Louis XVI trumeau mirror from Galerie Bazin was adapted to fit the space between the console and crown molding. Deniot notes that arched openings are architecturally dramatic and give rooms polish and power.

Opposite: Curtains by Romo in "Ravena" hang over sheer curtains by Dedar in "Stromboli." The horsehair fabric on the chairs is "Nircel" by Le Crin. Deniot says that a "neoclassical loft" was his concept for this open floor plan that incorporates the kitchen cabinet design into the dining room decor.

The color scheme of the apartment—an intricate interplay of black, ivory, grays, and cream—makes each detail quite emphatic, says the designer. "The apartment is a beautifully delineated 1,200 square feet, and all of the interior architecture is new. We had to redesign everything. We worked on it for two years, and I'm amazed at the amount of detail."

Deniot says that he can (almost) create decor for rooms with his eyes closed. But the interior architecture takes forever. "Balanced and harmonious interior architecture requires perfect proportions. Everything must be well executed," says Deniot. "I don't do blank rooms. My approach is very old-school. In the past, designers were involved with the architecture. When the architecture is perfected, and everything is logical and refined, the results are always better. I know where the electrical wiring should be for wall sconces, chandeliers, multiple lighting. I plan it."

With this approach he is able to conceal the alarm system, sound system, and A/C vents. When these basic, seemingly mundane services—and all other functional aspects—are perfectly placed, they are invisible. The interior is in order. It is elegant and polished. That's Deniot's stage for the decor.

"This apartment is lovely because it's on a very pretty little avenue, with a garden and the Eiffel Tower just outside the window," he says. "Now complete, it paints a portrait of a timeless French style, but without a period feeling."

In the vestibule, the arches open up the apartment, giving it volume and making its 1,200 square feet feel much larger. The nineteenth- century lanterns are from Galerie Vonthron, Paris. A set of twelve French black and white prints on paper is eighteenth century. Walls are faux-painted parchment in a special glazed finish technique. The newly installed antique oak floor was stained in a rosewood finish to match the doors.

Opposite: Kitchen hardware is by Deny Fontaine. The coffered ceiling was designed by Deniot, who created graphic and dramatic kitchen cabinets using glass fronts, paneling, and interior lighting.

A compact guest bedroom/office/study/dressing room has a 1940s André Arbus desk in fruitwood and ebony accents from Dominique Ilous, Marché Paul Bert, Saint-Ouen. The 1940s French Baguès nesting tables in faux bamboo finish are from On Site Antiques. The tailored sofa from Sean Cooper, UK, is covered with Georges Le Manach "Point de Tours" wool fabric. Custom-made pillows by Jean-François Lesage are embroidered with bronze thread. The toile patterned wall upholstery is in "Georges Sand" by Georges Le Manach. The alcove upholstery is a striped Brunschwig & Fils textile.

Opposite: In the master bedroom, with its soothing, monochromatic tones, the nineteenth-century French bed crown is from On Site Antiques. For simple, shimmering elegance, the brass Empire Amphora lamps are on 1810-period black marble bases from Jacques Maçon, France. The sound-reducing wall upholstery by Dedar in "Oxford" has two grosgrain ribbon trims designed to match the wood paneling below. A studded headboard was designed by Deniot. The headboard/bed cover is in "Croisillons" by Georges Le Manach.

The outside canopy is in wild silk by Jagtar, and the inside is "Sherin" by Zimmer + Rhode, with a fringe by Dedar. Deniot likes to apply silk velvet ribbons on wall upholstery to mimic French paneling.

INTO THE LIGHT:
A DRAMATIC REINVENTION

In early morning light, as Jean-Louis Deniot strolls along rue de Verneuil to his office, the narrow one-way street retains the village atmosphere captured a hundred years ago by photographers Charles Marville and Eugène Atget with their cumbersome camera equipment. Shuttered windows peer down, antique shop windows glimmer, and just a few cyclists animate the blurry maze of galleries.

"It's an eighteenth-century stone building, classical and typical for this antiques and art neighborhood," says Jean-Louis Deniot. "From the start, we renovated our offices in an effort to both retain and emphasize its eighteenth-century style."

The studios have become very eclectic: a mélange of exotic, eccentric, and elegant pieces accumulated through the years. Jean-Louis Deniot and his business partner, Virginie Deniot, acquired the compact space for their new office on rue de Verneuil in 2007. They recently expanded the studio to the second floor to accommodate management, the architecture team, the custom design department, and decorators. The Deniot team now numbers twenty.

The 3,700-square-foot workplace has rough stone walls that evoke a warm, residential feeling, but as an international headquarters it is also equipped with the latest technology. Everything is at hand, from files and the newest tech requirements, to fabric, carpet, tile, and stone samples.

For the new top floor of the building, Deniot added a skylight and a sculptural stairway, which had to be installed by crane. The interior is now dramatic—but to a passerby it remains discreet and hidden, suggesting its time-honored connection with the past.

In the entry, which is one of the original office rooms, wall lights are by Stilnovo. The Edwardian-style British leather armchairs and circular mirror are by Collection Pierre.

Opposite: Deniot decided to make a dramatic sculpture of the soaring double-height stair, and for emphasis, he added a collection of rather kinetic geometric abstract sculptures. The blue piece is from Denmark, 1960s. The ivory piece is a Los Angeles find from the 1970s. The dark bronze sculpture was custom designed by Deniot.

Following pages: The client sitting room offers harmonious symmetry as well as versatility for business and creative meetings. The coffee table is by Ado Chale, and the contemporary candlesticks are by Hervé Van der Straeten. Two vintage armchairs are in the style of Royère. The petite agate and gold side table is by Hiquily, with Picasso prints to the right. The mohair and silk rug is from Solstys.

The steel-reinforced skylight brightens the double-height stair landing and interior offices. To the right is the conference room. The encircling brass wall lights were designed by Deniot.

Opposite, top left: A hidden door behind faux books keeps clients' files confidential. A Louis XVI gilded bergère covered in handwoven cotton and wool fabric was brought by Deniot from Tangier. The chocolate shagreen tray side table is by R&Y Augousti. Top right: The Empire mahogany cylinder desk has been in Deniot's collection for several decades and holds pride of place in the office. It's a resting place for small bronze figures, petite lamps, or a Cire Trudon fragrant candle. The desk demonstrates Deniot's belief that large-scale furniture makes a small space appear bigger, and that an imposing antique bestows a certain grandeur and sense of architecture to a soft-spoken corner. The Maison Jansen ebonized chair is in the style of the Directoire period, and the 1950 painting is by John Marin. Bottom right: A lucite pedestal holds a Danish 1960 vase. The Louis XVI gilded sofa is covered in printed velvet from Lelièvre. The alabaster wall light is from Pouenat, and a bronze and glass side table is in the Fontana Arte style. Bottom left: A sculptural wall light is from Merlin, 1970 Paris Clignancourt flea market. A set of armchairs by Dominique in high gloss lacquer with brass accent is covered in Nya Nordiska fabric. Louis XVI armchairs with white patina have original black leather. An Atelier Prométhée neoclassical bronze glazed terra-cotta urn sits on a pedestal.

RIGHT BANK

Fine art, connoisseurship, antiques, fashion, and haute couture are signatures of the Right Bank. Fully immersed in this golden history-inflected arrondissement, Jean-Louis Deniot has created a super-luxe atmosphere for Chanel Haute Jouaillerie, and dreamed up a constellation of provocative decors for AD design showcases at Artcurial. In ultra-private apartments high above the throng, luscious custom-crafted sofas stand on artful handcrafted carpets, and architectural history is viewed and reviewed. Haussmann's grandeur and pomp are given a cool reappraisal, resulting in true elegance, harmony, and balance. Deniot rejects theme and period design, naturally, in favor of experimentation, daring, and lavish luxe.

AN ETHEREAL PLAY OF COLOR

A brief walk from Place du Trocadéro, and with the Eiffel Tower looming in the sky across the Seine, avenue d'Eylau is an elegant and leafy respite from the onrush of Parisian traffic beyond. The avenue is broad, and grand stone mansions on each side feel discreet and untouched since they were built in the late nineteenth century, under the influence of Baron Georges-Eugène Haussmann.

This powerful prefect of the Seine district was commissioned by Napoleon III to create a new Paris of grand boulevards and open spaces, lined with handsome classical residences. Their highly codified silhouettes, fenestration, adornments, and stone exteriors — classic Paris of today — all ensure uniformity, harmony, and a consistent cityscape.

But, as Jean-Louis Deniot notes, this fast and furious rebuilding also left the city with many mediocre buildings and pompous facades with interiors that were often a hodge-podge of styles. The second-rate materials and plaster-happy decoration, says Deniot, were repeated from one building to the next. He has seen hundreds in his fifteen-year career.

As an architect, Jean-Louis Deniot creates perfectly balanced interior architecture that has spirit, elegance, and harmony. In the hallway he created the look of floor-to-ceiling pilasters by raising fluted moldings up into the ceiling cove. This also makes the walls seem higher, the ceiling more graceful. Floor-to-ceiling limestone plaster and coffee-colored marble floors make for an elegant entry hall.

The twentieth-century painted metal banquettes, covered in a tweed fabric by Zimmer + Rohde, are from On Site Antiques. A pair of sculptural 1960s sconces by Gio Ponti is from Galerie Jean Pierre Orinel. The 1980s console with a smoked mirror top is from Dominique Ilous. The 1950s ceramic and wood lamp is from On Site Antiques, and the custom-made lampshade is by Anne Sokolsky. The quartet of 1950s brushed copper and wood Danish suspension lights, attributed to Holm Sorensen and Co., Denmark, is from Galerie Jean Pierre Orinel. Deniot notes that highly polished dark marble (here coffee stone) paired with glossy doors and large windows gives an ethereal, light-reflecting, and uplifting effect to a room.

The three-bedroom apartment is now an ode to gray. "Gray has been a signature color of Paris for centuries and is a particular favorite of mine," says the designer. "Gray can be cold and somewhat drab, which is not automatically terrible. But it can be so dreamy and romantic—fresh, elegant, and full of life. It can have tones of blue or green, even yellow, or it can be that particular Parisian gray that is a little bit green with a drop of ocher—and I find it chic and lighthearted. Gray is a color that has to be adapted and custom-designed for the light in each room," he says. He may sometimes start with dove gray, or a very soft mouselike gray. He recently painted the walls of a chateau near Paris in a warm charcoal gray, with soft-white plaster trim.

"We always put many samples, large swathes of paint, on the walls and look at them in all lights, including candlelight" says the designer. "It is important to check and adjust gray, depending on the paint texture and the natural light."

Deniot and his team may have as many as three or four different grays in a room—perhaps a paler gray on walls, a darker gray on moldings, and another tone on perhaps a lacquer door, so that ultimately the decor is a calmly composed adagio of color, with no tone predominating. He enthusiastically chooses gray in fabrics as well—upholstering chairs or sofas in complex gray tweeds, dressing beds in soft gray baby alpaca weaves, and working with Galerie Diurne for art-inspired multi-gray patterns for carpets. For Deniot, gray is a go-to color, his hue for all seasons.

"I mix and use only custom colors," says the designer. "I mix a bit of the tints and palette of one into each room color so that they all relate and feel harmonious. It's a discreet way of using paint, and feels serene and low-key in decor. I do this mix with all colors, including white."

The living room of the 2,800-square-foot apartment was reinvented and pared down. All specious period details were replaced with simplified paneling and dentil molding. "The living room was once topped with a frilly crown molding," says Deniot. Now it's more sleek Ruhlman, more Paris salon. The 1950s curved sofas with tubular feet in polished brass by Marco Zanuso from Cyril Grizot were recovered in custom-designed tweed by Deniot.

Previous pages: In all of his interiors, Deniot works with French craftsmen and often uses arcane techniques that were fashionable in the 1930s. The overscale coffee table decorated in intricate straw marquetry is by Lison de Caunes, custom designed by Deniot. It's crisp and glimmering, with a nod to French art deco taste. The large carpet was custom made with a random geometric pattern by Galerie Diurne. "I introduced various shades of gray and ivory into this cubist custom rug to serve as a structural background to the many shapes of furniture," says Deniot.

The fireplace, with a nod to Jean-Michel Frank, is handcrafted in shimmering mica in tones of natural brown and gray. The faceted octagonal mirror above the fireplace is by Deniot. In contrast, two lamps on the drum side tables are in metal and cement, by Mathilde Pénicaud with custom-made lampshades by Anne Sokolsky. To the right of the fireplace, the 1960s–70s lacquered ivory buffet is by Guy Lefèvre for Jansen. Like a piece of jewelry in the corner, the 1950s lamp on the buffet is black opalescent ceramic, in the style of Jouve, from On Site Antiques. The 1950 armchairs from On Site Antiques were recovered in "Brooklyn 3210/02" by Jim Thompson. For an airy effect, the curtain was custom designed by Deniot. The metal floor lamp, a grace note on the gray paneling, is by Pietro Chiesa.

"Everyone speaks with awe about Haussmann, but in reality, most of the interiors are extremely banal, with little sign of individuality or style," says Deniot, who recently completed new interiors for one such Haussmann mansion. The residence had been acquired by an international couple, based in London, with three young children. They come and go, sometimes for weekends, and in summer for longer sojourns.

"I discussed concepts in detail with my clients, and it was obvious that major reconstruction would result in a much more gracious, spacious, and truly chic interior," says Deniot. "First to go were the 'gateau à la crème' plaster crown moldings and the cliché fake Louis XV fireplaces. Then the old doors had to be dismantled." Deniot's full-scope reinvention of the rooms included creating new floors and raising the header of all doors.

Today the rooms look as if they were always so beautifully proportioned, with ten-foot-tall double doors finished with ten coats of lacquer and custom hardware. Plain and as reflective as mirrors, they add flashes of light and modernity throughout the apartment.

"We restructured walls and installed steel beams for support in order to get the doors from seven to ten feet," Deniot says. Now, plain paneled walls throw into high relief the collections of sculptures and paintings. Furniture scooped up in Antwerp, Los Angeles, and hidden corners of Paris gives the rooms energy and a very modern kind of offhand chic.

"Everything from the art to the dining chairs, the graphic new lighting and the overscale custom-made straw-marquetry coffee table feels current, and it's lighthearted," he says. "For a young family, there is no reason to be overly reverent to design history. And it was tailored just for them."

In the dining room, the suspension light is "Lustre Module" from Hervé Van der Straeten in chocolate patinated bronze and brass polished nickel. Charmingly individual, the almost kinetic 1950s walnut chairs attributed to Franco Campo and Carlo Graffi were traced at a Pierre Bergé sale in Belgium. The straw marquetry tabletop in the living room echoes the dining room's wall upholstery. Deniot custom designed the stained mahogany table and the parchment and wood sideboard. The painting is by Philip Guston. The white biscuit lamp is from Jean-Michel Merlin with a shade by Anne Sokolsky. The dark lacquered doors paired with silver linen wall upholstery bring added shine when evening candles are lit.

Previous pages: The living room and dining room were designed as an ensemble, with more pronounced brown and taupe tones in the dining room. In the living room alcoves, a pair of 1950s sconces in patinated metal by Gino Sarfatti is from Alexander Goult, Paris. The wood sculpture in the left alcove is *Personnage Cadac*, by Parvine Curie and the bronze sculpture in the right alcove is *Le Chevalier* by Maxime Adam-Tessier, both from Galerie Yves Gastou.

In the kitchen and breakfast room, the 1950 varnished walnut table is by Paul Frankl. White opaline 1960s pendant lights are a lighthearted party decoration. A pair of bronze candleholders is by Hervé Van der Straeten, and the large graphic sculpture *Grail 1* is from Domani.

The dramatic central wall and door (built into the decor) were crafted in Constructivist stainless steel matt-brushed plates. For Deniot, harmony and clarity are key. He concealed kitchen appliances using a stainless steel back wall and minimized rigidity with a set of vintage pendants.

The 1950s black-stained walnut chairs by Paul Frankl are covered in woven Italian leather from Garrett Leather. Suave and chic, the taupe stained oak flooring by Parquets Briatte is matched with the taupe stone on kitchen work surfaces. The banquette is in hardwearing horsehair from Zimmer + Rhode. "A horsehair banquette perched at the end of a kitchen island can create a space-saving breakfast area or a casual dining room," says Deniot.

Following pages: In the study, a 1950 walnut and gold-leaf coffee table was acquired in Los Angeles. A glamorous accessory, the metal and glass 1950s ceiling light is by Fontana Arte. Curtains are in a Dedar fabric. Cubist shapes energize the custom-made rug by Galerie Diurne. The sofa from Pierre Frey is covered in fabric by Le Manach. Above it is a 1970 brushed brass piece in relief by Miroslav Brozek from Galerie Régis Royant. Walls are covered in custom-colored leather panels from Le QR. Deniot notes that playful texturing, such as palm-tree-wood cabinetry and large leather-tile panels, brings a masculine, cigar-box feeling to the room.

The master bedroom is serene and welcoming when the owners arrive from London. Everything is luxurious and precise. The custom-made headboard is upholstered in Westbury Textiles "Portofino." The 1950 nightstands in black lacquered birch wood by Heywood-Wakefield are from Galerie D'Agata. The gilded metal bedside lights from Jean Pierre Orinel are from the 1970s, with shades by Anne Sokolsky. The custom hand-sewn bedcover in baby alpaca is by Alta Pampa. The rug designed by Jean-Louis Deniot was custom made by Galerie Diurne.

A pair of 1960 armchairs by Ramos from Galerie Régis Royant is covered in fabric from Kvadrat. The sculpted gueridon by Hiquily is from Galerie Yves Gastou. A chandelier in resin from Pouenat is named "Last Night." The 1970s large round mirror in rosewood and gold leaf is from Galerie Jean Pierre Orinel. Walls are in a decorative paint with a faux parchment effect. In bedrooms, says Deniot, a panoramic headboard offers an expansive effect in addition to a frame for nightstands.

Following pages: The custom-made hammered brass fireplace was designed by Deniot. The 1950s brass articulated lamp from Stilnovo with a lacquered metal lampshade is from On Site Antiques. A jewelry-like custom bronze fireplace provides a feminine touch, says Deniot.

Deniot travels to India often, working on projects in Delhi, Mumbai, Chandigarh, Chennai, and Simla. Marble has long been used as a cool material in the hot Indian climate. Here, the marble walls and floors, with stone from Carrara, were detailed by Deniot. Only the moldings are painted in faux marbre. The 1960 metal light suspension, "Moon," is by Verner Panton. Wall lights in silver leaf are by Hervé Van der Straeten. Bathroom fittings are from Dornbracht.

In one of the kids' rooms, the nightstand is by Julian Chichester. Dramatic and sinuous, the Hiquily brass lamp is from Yves Gastou. The wall sculpture is by Curtis Jere, whose work, made in Southern California, is now very collectible and a lighthearted favorite of Deniot.

The headboard and side armchair are covered in Le Manach fabric. A custom bolster and bedspread are in alpaca by Alta Pampa. "Strong graphics against a sleek background should be used in small doses," says Deniot. "I like a hint of brass to introduce a sunny dimension in a small bedroom." The 2003 painting, *Large City Scape* by Peyret, is from Galerie Régis Royant.

IMAGINATION SET FREE

Jean-Louis Deniot took the chic Parisian art crowd on an imaginary voyage with his dramatic gallery presentation for AD Interieurs 2012 at Artcurial, the antiques and art auction headquarters.

In the inventive showcase design, which included a monochromatic ivory vestibule and a smoky topaz living room, all perspectives are abstract and exaggerated, all surfaces deliberately blurring proportion and logical balance. Antique mirror, laser-cut wood panels, gold-leaf bronze, and shimmering fabrics heighten the intergalactic journey. Visitors could sense a two-or three-dimensional effect, a sensory delight.

"It's a poetic, dreamy, surrealistic decor, as I intended, and I had so much fun putting it all together with no limits," says Deniot.

This was a chance to cast aside his classical training and his elegant, restrained, and superbly polished neoclassical work. "Every element of the architecture, materials, and furnishing was extreme, to the max."

Deniot's installation was a space odyssey, literally out of this world with virtuoso techniques, daring swoops of the imagination, and an exploration of ideas without boundaries. Each surface offered new materials and techniques, hallucinatory effects, a new definition of luxury, craft, visual delight, and chic.

In the entry, backlit paneling, laser cut and lacquered, was designed by Deniot and manufactured by CEMAD. The "Metal Blade" console of oxidized brass was designed by Deniot and manufactured in Morocco. The mirror frame in patinated plaster and the cubist plaster lamp were designed by Deniot and manufactured by Atelier Prométhée, France. The lampshade was custom made by Anne Sokolsky.

Following pages: In the living room, wall upholstery fabric, "Soie Sauvage" by IDO, was manufactured in Thailand. The chimneypiece of inlaid antique mirror was designed by Deniot and made by Gottardo, France. The sculpted cotton carpet was custom designed by Deniot and manufactured by Tai Ping, China.

The rooms came together over three months, an extraordinary achievement considering the international scope of the project. Linara "Peppercorn" linen and cotton "Romo" fabric were used for the custom-made sofas in five shaded tones by Romo, Italy. Jean-Louis Deniot designed the structure (manufactured by Jean de Merry) to replicate the carpet pattern by Tai Ping. The sheer window shade was embroidered with beads of bone, wood, strips of raffia, bronze thread, parchment, and leather thread to a design by Deniot. The embroidery by Jean-François Lesage was handcrafted by specialists in India. The earthenware 1930s vase on the coffee table is from On Site Antiques. The chandelier of patinated brass and parchment by Deniot was custom made by Ombre Portée, France.

The endlessly fascinating showcase concept offered Deniot the freedom to experiment, dream, and go on his own imaginary journey. He especially enjoyed working with the artists who custom crafted these one-of-a-kind elements. The large oak sculpture, *Red Gum Sheaves*, and the medium oak sculpture, *Enclosed Slices Column*, both with stands in patinated, oxidized brass, are by David Nash. The polished brass reading lamp, opposite, was designed by Deniot and manufactured in Morocco, with a custom lampshade by Anne Sokolsky. The decorative painted glass partition is by Florence Girette.

Previous pages: Deniot refined the color scheme to tones of taupe, smoky topaz, bronze, putty, and ivory. The Jean de Merry coffee table in Plexiglas and polished brass mimics the carpet's pattern. David Nash's cast iron *Cross Egg* sits atop the coffee table.

"The initial concept was to portray a maximum of richness and opulence, with lots of gold and sumptuous materials, but in the most contemporary way possible," says Deniot.

In classical decor, every millimeter has a specific treatment, finish, and pattern. In this space, the accumulation of different effects—mirror, silk, embroidery, plaster, linen, steel, crystal, carved wood—provides a sense of lushness to the decor. Deniot called the approach "contemporary maximalism."

"I designed the decor as an artistic interior installation," he says. The complexity of the composition and the juxtaposition of scale were the key: to have mass, space, volume, shadow, light, contrast, and direct dialogues between the interior architecture and furnishing."

The concept behind using the same off-balance patterns in various scales was to limit the cacophony.

"As well as the ethnic and imaginary notions behind my theme, I included pieces manufactured in more than a dozen different countries to represent my love of travel, different destinations, and local craftsmanship." The sofas were manufactured by Jean de Merry in Los Angeles and are covered in six different Italian linens to create shadows and accentuate movement. He embroidered fabrics in India and crafted metal pieces in northern Morocco. Fragments of the same motif are found in the sixty-eight intricate pieces of distressed bronze and parchment for the extravagant chandelier.

An overscale fireplace covered in mosaics of distressed mirror was developed using the cubist motif on yet another scale. Jean-François Lesage, based in Chennai, India, crafted a large window screen, embroidered with leather laces, bone pearls, raffia, parchment appliqués, and bronze thread. The backlit wooden paneling in the vestibule—also cubist and abstract—was manufactured to include three layers, with recessed volumes, cutouts, and projections.

A CHANGE IN ELEVATION

Avenue Montaigne, in the eighth arrondissement just off the Champs-Elysées, is bordered with illustrious fashion houses (Dior, Chanel, Bottega Veneta), the top-drawer Hôtel Plaza-Athénée, and international jewelers. The broad, sycamore-shaded avenue is lovely for leafy views and close to theatres, an art deco cinema, and chic restaurants, all within a stiletto stroll.

In this privileged neighborhood, Jean-Louis Deniot's clients found their apartment in a 1930s art deco building. Paris was building fast in the 1930s, and the Moderne style was the architecture of choice. Sometimes its themes of geometric framing and simplified detailing were carried into the interiors.

"There was some vestigial sense of Paris 1930s in the apartment, so we decided to go in that direction," says the designer. "We used art deco as an influence, with a hint of neoclassicism."

Deniot created a sense of architecture, stature, and volume with grooved pilasters in plaster. At the end of the entry foyer, above the iron console designed by Deniot for Pouenat and dubbed "Homere," is an artwork by Damien Hirst. To give a feeling of depth and substance to the rather open white space, plaster urns from Carole Gratale, USA, were placed on square columns in straw marquetry designed by Deniot. But there's a lighthearted touch, with a pair of lamps in bronze on marble bases by Hervé Van der Straeten.

The classic Jean-Michel Frank–style desk is in light oak and parchment. The chairs are a custom upholstery of production pieces from Mise en Demeure, Paris. "I added the new vertical pilasters to give the room an instant axial dimension," says Deniot. "Entries can often be simply a 'pass-through' space, and I wanted the foyer to feel interesting, atmospheric, and surprising."

Above: This detail includes a fossil by Claude de Muzac from Galerie Yves Gastou, a shagreen vase from R&Y Augousti, and a 1930s vase from On Site Antiques.

Deniot selected fine reproductions for the apartment, rather than the one-of-a-kind, custom-made furniture he specifies in most of his work. "I've always admired Baker's fantastic way of interpreting great classical styles in a sleek, timeless version, and with superb craftsmanship," he says. "The designs have personality and integrity. The Baker pieces I selected for the living room were ideal for this apartment, which needed a fine-tuned and soft sensibility."

Deniot wanted clean lines—and not too many antique pieces. "My clients did not want a lot of vintage, so we gave it a wonderfully polished look with the Baker pieces. I was very pleased with this look," he says. The new interior architecture, with a series of columns and bold ceiling coffers, makes an interesting counterpoint to Baker's designs. "We also used McGuire production pieces in the kitchen, with great success. I love the character of these rattan designs, and in this setting they're very fresh."

Armchairs from Christopher Guy are covered in "Aspen" and a decorative pillow is covered in "Mirage Check," both by Jim Thompson. The custom-designed daybed by Deniot is covered in a Beacon Hill textile. The Pierre Barbion sculpture is from Galerie Yves Gastou. The custom crown molding and coffered ceiling is by Deniot, who notes that perspective can be a decisive element in room design. When cleverly exploited, it can convert door-frames and the view beyond into a virtual still-life painting.

Previous pages: A silk and wool rug is from Gallery Diurne. The stool in bronze and brass, "Heros," was designed by Deniot for Pouenat and covered in Pierre Frey velvet. The desk chair from Ironies, USA, is covered in Jim Thompson fabric. The bronze and light oak desk is from Christian Liaigre. A convertible sofa from Collection Pierre is covered in Pierre Frey "Moustier." The wall tapestry by Pablo Picasso is from J. Pansu. The wood paneling with leather insert wall concept was designed by Deniot. The lantern, "Cyclope," was designed by Deniot for Pouenat. Among the few vintage pieces is a 1940s black leather armchair by André Arbus from Galerie Yves Gastou. Deniot designed the articulated overhead lights. He notes that sharp contrasts, such as crisp trim against leather walls, can transform a room's atmosphere. The library's mood is achieved by not using traditional natural wood finishes.

Pages 172–73: In the living room, the custom-designed coffee table is by Deniot, and the silk rug is from Gallery Diurne. Deniot loves contrast and discreet materials—he selected shagreen candlesticks and a tray and box from R & Y Augousti, Paris. The sofa from Baker is covered in Colefax & Fowler fabric with leather piping. The decorative pillow is from Prelle. The Jean-Michel Frank–style cabinet is in ebony and parchment. The sculpture by Yerassimos Sklavos is from Galerie Yves Gastou. The wallpaper is Romo's "Eggshell Stone." Says Deniot, "A partition wall can take on a graphic and sculptural form in juxtaposition to a neutral color palette. Here it serves also to divide the hall and the living room."

In comparison with the bustling avenue beyond the windows, the bedroom is calm, understated, and beautifully composed. Above the bed is *Mask (Face Station)*, 2011, by Matthew Monahan, in fiberglass, epoxy resin, gold leaf, and wood. Deniot added to the composed feeling with wall upholstery in Jim Thompson silk.

The custom headboard is covered in Hodsoll McKenzie "Bamboo Twill." The custom-designed bench by Deniot is covered in Boussac "Andreas Blanc." The new mirror, "Achille," was designed by Deniot for Pouenat. The multi-level jewelry box in shagreen is from R & Y Augousti. The alabaster lamp is from Vaughan, with a 1940s Murano glass chandelier. The alpaca bedcover is from Alta Pampa.

The kitchen gains a design spin from the chandelier, "Helios," designed by Deniot for Pouenat. The black lacquered rattan chairs are from McGuire. The table is from Baker, USA. To prevent a seating nook from feeling claustrophobic, Deniot designs mirrors and wood-trimmed walls to echo an already introduced pattern.

Opposite: In the guest bedroom, the silk rug is from Gallery Diurne, Paris. To soften sound Deniot chose interlined curtains in Pierre Frey "Moustier" with contrast borders in Jim Thompson "Legend." He feels that curtain fabric with a contrasting border trim is the secret to avoiding plain designs. Providing a sculptural accent is the iron armchair, "Ulysse," designed by Deniot for Pouenat, covered in Pierre Frey indigo blue mohair velvet. The lamp from Porta Romana stands on a desk from Birgit Israel, London.

Deniot often creates a niche to surround a bed, by inserting new closets at each side. This gives a room architecture, while hiding clothing and bed linen storage. The baby alpaca bedspread is by Alta Pampa. The custom-designed nightstands are in light oak and parchment. The silk wallpaper from Philip Jeffries is "Elephant Mosaique."

ELEGANCE AND SUPER-LUXE

Jean-Louis Deniot completed a dream assignment for Chanel: creating a Ritz hotel suite in homage to Coco Chanel, using her style and design codes as references. The Place Vendôme suite would be a background for the presentation of Chanel's *haute joaillerie* (luxury jewels) and a setting to celebrate the legends and traditions of Chanel herself.

"I decided not to be too literal, too imitative," says Deniot. "With just a few subtle motifs, colors, and a dash of intrigue, I wanted to suggest Chanel rather than make a snapshot or paint her portrait. The white peacock, for example, from the famous taxidermy gallery Deyrolle, alludes to the grace and femininity of Chanel."

Deniot commissioned a dramatic sunburst mirror from Paris designer/jeweler/artist Hervé Van der Straeten in recognition of the many artists—among them Salvador Dali, Paul Iribe, Pablo Picasso, Alberto Giacometti, and the ubiquitous Jean Cocteau—who inspired and worked closely with Chanel on the decor of her apartment and her boutiques. Her favorite artists also created many of her signature jewelry designs.

Deniot created an oneiric setting to honor Coco Chanel's legendary rue Cambon apartment "above the shop" and her Ritz pied-à-terre. Chanel lived for many years at the Ritz. Deniot placed an armful of luxurious white roses in a crystal vase on the suite's balcony overlooking the Napoleon I column, as Chanel did when she lived in the hotel, in the chic heart of Paris.

The sleek white peacock, above, is from Deyrolle, the centuries-old rue du Bac naturalist/taxidermist. The rock crystal chandelier is from Mathieu Lustrerie. Jean-Louis Deniot chose the plaster wall lights as a reference to surreal film set designs by Coco Chanel's ubiquitous collaborator and friend, Jean Cocteau. The large custom bronze mirror frame hovers over the original fireplace along with the white peacock, echoing Chanel's *haute joaillerie* feather diamond brooch.

Deniot designed a high-gloss lacquered table with backlit quartz and a plaster base in the style of Jean-Charles Moreux and Serge Roche. The rock crystals (another of Chanel's favorite devices) create an alluring background for a new collection of Chanel's high-jewelry diamonds.

Opposite: Two LaLanne bronze doe sculptures are from Coco Chanel's apartment on rue Cambon. The room feels nocturnal, mysterious, and glamorous, with edges dissolving into darkness. The polygonal mirror was custom designed by Jean-Louis Deniot with a hexagonal center echoing the Place Vendôme's layout.

Previous pages: Every move, each motif, and all silhouettes are in homage to the iconic Chanel interiors on rue Cambon. The sun mirror is by Hervé Van der Straeten, and the satin sofa is by Collection Pierre. The club armchair by Jean-Michel Frank sits upon a handcrafted Nepalese wool rug by Galerie Diurne and alongside a plaster floor lamp designed by Deniot. The side chair and desk are by Emilio Terry. Floor pillows in suede were embroidered by Jean-François Lesage. Deniot designed the silk screens to suggest the 1930s Coco Chanel era. The black custom-designed mother-of-pearl coffee table was made after a model drawn by Christian Bérard representing Coco Chanel in her suite. The custom rock crystal bonsai was designed by Deniot in honor of Chanel's extravagant tastes.

OPTIC VERVE

When the editor of French *Architectural Digest*, Marie Kalt, invited the top twelve French designers to dream up interiors to showcase art at Artcurial, the prestigious auction house on the Champs-Elysées, Jean-Louis Deniot was selected to design and produce a concept. Designers were offered a series of bare corporate spaces and given carte blanche.

"My idea was reminiscent of all that is galactic, solar, orbital: the Milky Way, craters, minerals, energies, nebulae, and constellations while evoking infinity, dreams, and poetic contemplation," says Deniot.

His vision (free from the conventional client constraints) was a grand sweep of the past and future of French design, without a scintilla of nostalgia or reverence. Its assured elegance and confident panache radiate updated, re-booted, twenty-first-century glamour.

Deniot seized on iconic art works, thematic collections, and collaborations with artists. This was ephemeral decor (it was on view for only two weeks) to inspire emotion and provoke a reaction from the viewer, says the designer.

Custom-made doorframes manufactured in hammered and distressed brass add a raw and precious dimension to the space. Wall upholstery fabrics by Jim Thompson and Pierre Frey featuring an agate/onyx motif were selected by Deniot to bring an organic effect to the space. Deniot added crown molding to create an architectural effect. The seventeenth-century marble busts on marble plinths are from Galerie Steinitz, Paris, and side armchairs were designed by Deniot for Collection Pierre. The 1950 giant ceramic lamp is from On Site Antiques.

The playful lights by Ombre Portée were hung on the floating ceiling to give a sense of spatial grace and movement. The console by Mathilde Pénicaud for 3eme Rue Galerie, above, reflects the art theme. The elaborate seventeenth-century French mirror is from the illustrious Galerie Steinitz, Paris.

Eclectic works of art and custom design, brutalist and luxurious materials, remarkable antiques, and extraordinary embroideries all created in Deniot's hand a silken and cohesive menagerie of exceptional craftsmanship. His dazzle of rare objects—geodes, minerals, gold-leaf metal "sea urchins"—is simultaneously contemporary and vintage.

"I saw and built the design on the scale of a Parisian apartment," says the designer.

There's jousting between proportion and composition, and almost kinetic contrasts such as mineral and mechanical, freeform and geometric, rough and smooth, shiny and matt, suppleness and brutalism. It's Deniot at his freest.

The crystals, above, are from Jean-Louis Deniot's private collection. The mirror, opposite, was designed by Jean-Louis Deniot for the Artcurial showcase. Crafted by Pouenat Ferronnier, the twelve-foot-tall piece is composed of distressed mirror with tonalities of bronze and silver, framed with a large, bright brass border. The mirror also boasts twenty ornate spiky bronze "stars" on the surface to add a poetic and three-dimensional element.

Previous pages: The lacquered constructivist screens were designed by Deniot to compose an octagonal entry hall. Four large-scale plaster lamps were designed to add a grand, monumental effect to the space. Deniot was inspired by the works of Alberto Giacometti and Georges Jouve, a 1940s ceramic artist, to bring a playful, exaggerated, freeform element to the pieces. The vestibule wall paneling, including the tone-on-tone colors, was designed by Deniot in homage to Mondrian for this Artcurial designer showcase. All the panels are raised to add a sense of substance and volume with a curve at the top, creating a large cove crown. Wall-to-wall carpet manufactured by Codimat was designed by Jean-Louis Deniot to play with dimensions, and to mix up the vertical and the horizontal. The chandelier is "Gravitations N°385," in bronze with engraved glass wings by Hervé Van der Straeten.

Opposite: In the vestibule, the center table by Brussels artist/designer Ado Chale is from Galerie Yves Gastou. This one-of-a-kind table has a curious bronze top, which references the moon's surface. The large, custom-made silk window screen was designed by Deniot with exquisite embroidery in wool tweed, silver and bronze thread, glass sequins, and linen by Jean-François Lesage. Curule seating, inspired by ancient Roman examples, is by Deniot for Collection Pierre. It is upholstered in fabric by Pierre Frey and embellished by Jean-François Lesage using bronze nail heads and brass sequins in silhouettes based on Deniot's astrology signs, Virgo and Scorpio.

The large bronze sculpture, *Les Ailes* by Stahly, is from Galerie Yves Gastou. On the wall is Untitled (2006) by Gerwald Rockenschaub, from Galerie Thaddaeus Ropac. This piece represents a dream island and includes teal lacquered Lucite and stainless steel.

PARIS WEEKENDS

Paris is engaging, fascinating, and inspiring, and so naturally on weekends (starting with a fast Friday getaway) hard-working professionals like Jean-Louis Deniot must escape to the green world of historic French forests. Friday afternoons it's time to pack the car boot with Champagne, design magazines, cashmere sweaters, and Wellingtons. A one-hour car trip takes the designer and friends into the former hunting grounds of Louis XV. It's an exceptionally lush region, with noble ancient oaks that are considered national treasures, and castles and palatial stables that bespeak past grandeur. And further to the southwest, a longer drive, equally verdant, takes Virginie Deniot and her family into the Touraine.

THE PERFECT FRENCH COUNTRY HOUSE

Hidden behind a moss-covered stone wall and a flourish of noble beech, oak, and elm trees, the handsome turreted 1820 limestone residence could hardly be more discreet.

This is where Jean-Louis Deniot retreats on Friday evenings, driving north from Paris in the darkening twilight. All is silent as he navigates country roads, where nearby stables exercise their horses.

When Deniot arrives, he takes a few minutes to light fires in the library, dining room, and living room and to set a match to mint-scented Abd el Kader candles in the foyer. The candles burn all weekend, giving the interiors a romantic, evocative mood.

This seven-bedroom Chantilly house is now ready to welcome a lively horde of friends, who arrive from London, Delhi, or New York in a tumble of dogs and luggage for a weekend of late dinners, dancing, and frolic. It's an ultra-private setting for laughter, intense conversations, and relaxation. And Deniot's décor, with dramatic Hervé Van der Straeten chandeliers, cashmere-covered sofas, soft lighting, dreamy beds, and old-world charm, is a magical setting.

In the tile-floored vestibule, an eighteenth-century Portuguese settee is covered in embossed Lelièvre mohair velvet. Early-eighteenth-century Spanish plant stands are wrought iron. The French lantern is mid-nineteenth century. The curtains are Pierre Frey natural linen. Deniot created a leafy transitional ambiance in the entry with the Portuguese lacelike carved sofa paired with two standing plants of the same palette and the scenic window view framed in linen. The tiles are original to the house.

Opposite: The Chantilly house, with its whimsical decorative turrets, is surrounded by ten acres of green velvet lawns. Spring-fed streams crisscross the ten-acre property.

Deniot's concept for the historic house was to first get the backgrounds right—that's his mantra. Plaster walls were painted, and some were covered with textured wallpaper or simple cotton textiles. He painted some wood floors matt black but left the original patterned tile floor in the foyer untouched. It looks as if it was decorated with treasures over many decades, rather than the few years of Deniot's subtle tweaks and improvements.

"The plan was to decorate with a mix of vintage pieces and antiques, along with traditional fabrics—wool, natural linen, silk—so that the house looks as if it has always stayed in the same family," he explains. Today it appears as if the next generation has kept favorite heirlooms, updating and adding over time with favorite flea market finds, newly commissioned sculptured lighting, and treasures of today.

The sunny study becomes a gathering point for cocktails and fireside conversation after dark. A pair of 1950s slipper chairs from On Site Antiques is covered in John Hutton wool fabric. The vintage Moroccan rug was purchased in Asilah, northern Morocco. The Coco Chanel–style sofa is covered in Romo "Rumba" fabric. Decorative pillows have metallic Dédar trim appliqués. The black opaline-top coffee table is 1940s, and custom bookcases are gold-leaf forged iron. The portrait is French, seventeenth century.

Custom woven wool curtains were manufactured in Scotland. Deniot likes a combination of woven wool, alpaca, and cashmere fabrics and rugs in natural tones to give a warm, traditional feeling to the study/library. The black leather 1960 Danish armchair is by Borge Mogensen. The decorative pillow is from Zimmer + Rohde. On the oak mantel, alabaster globe lamps are juxtaposed with a black ebony vase and a contemporary Hervé Van der Straeten bronze-framed mirror with bronze twigs.

Deniot's collections of "high" and "low" include an elegant 1880 black marble clock mixed with a pair of bronze candlesticks that were on sale at Pottery Barn. The black and white photo is by Karl Lagerfeld. The colonial-era African wooden elephant, early twentieth century, is in ebony.

In the living room, the Baguès for Maison Jansen coffee table is Chinese lacquer. Two articulated reading lamps in patinated brass with a metal shade are from Van Baggum Collecties, a design firm in the Netherlands. Chairs in front of the fireplace are from Marc Philippe. Prints on the walls are from Rome. The rug in sea grass was custom made by Crucial Trading.

Opposite: In a corner of the living room, the nineteenth-century column is in patinated gilt wood. The vase, perhaps formerly a stage prop, is enameled sandstone. The Napoleon III armchair and Louis XIV sofas are covered in Lelièvre mohair velvet. The Napoleon III sofa, also covered in Lelièvre mohair velvet, was a lucky find from Marché Paul-Bert at the Clignancourt flea market. The pillow on the sofa is by Fortuny.

Previous pages: The chaise by Frédéric Méchiche for First Time is covered in a pearl gray and butter-toned striped silk taffeta from Jim Thompson. A 1940 Baguès chandelier in crystal and gilt bronze is from Marc Philippe. The late-nineteenth-century Chinese pedestal table is in dark wood. Deniot's deft wall design uses different shades of gray to perform different functions. Here the dark gray provides depth to the plaster center panels, while the medium gray accentuates both verticality and definition. The lighter gray provides crisp contrast.

A nineteenth-century mirror and English chest of drawers are in Chinese lacquer. Chairs from Jansen are covered in velvet from Rubelli. Gold, in a modulated dosage, says Deniot, makes decor sing. "Don't be afraid of chandeliers and glitter in the country," he says. "They provide contrast. Their glamour is shown to advantage with more rustic decor as a counterpoint."

The late-nineteenth-century terra-cotta sculpture was found at a Chantilly antique shop. Striped wallpaper is from Farrow & Ball. To prevent a large lampshade from becoming overpowering on a tablescape, says Deniot, it should match rather than contrast with the wall color.

Opposite: The impact of the massive red marble Louis XIV–style fireplace is softened by bark-patterned wall fabric from Pasaya, Paris, in a similar russet color. The Maison Jansen high-gloss-top Louis XV–style dining table was custom made in the 1940s. The 1940s French chairs were covered in Nobilis Paris horsehair. The floor-mounted overscale mirror with bronze sea urchin appliqués was designed by Deniot for the Pouenat collection. The virtuoso rock crystal and gold-bronze chandelier was designed by Hervé Van der Straeten. The gold-framed portrait is Louis XVI period.

In the sunny master bedroom, which has an adjacent open terrace, the custom headboard and bed canopy frame were designed by Jean-Louis Deniot. The designer notes that a wooden crown molding suspended from the ceiling can give the dramatic look of a more formal four-poster canopy bed. The rust silk is from Jim Thompson, striped wallpaper is from Farrow & Ball, and chocolate brown mohair pillows are from Lelièvre.

Opposite: To modulate the all-white effect of the Jacob Delafon tub, Deniot painted it taupe, red, and gray. The antique Indian silver chairs, bought on 1stdibs.com, were covered in red cashmere from Pierre Frey. Towel racks and fixtures in shiny nickel are from Volevatch. Cotton towels are from Ralph Lauren. Taffeta curtains are from Métaphore, with Mokuba ribbon trim.

"A bathroom can be inventive, playful, and sometimes a little eccentric," says Deniot. "This is a weekend house, so there is time to linger in the bathtub in the morning or relax at the end of the day. In this bathroom, with views of the treetops, the bathtub has been positioned at the center to enjoy both the garden and the fireplace view. It's also very nice for reading a book or listening to music."

The dining room has seen many celebrations, including birthdays, engagements, visits by friends from afar, Christmas, and New Year's Eve, as well as impromptu late-evening summer feasting.

In the middle of winter, with snow flurries turning the landscape a ghostly monochrome, fires burn throughout the house, including in the dining room. Clustered beeswax candles are lit on the mantel and along the center of the dining table.

The newest adornments of the dining room include an exceptionally glamorous gold-leaf bronze chandelier with shimmering faceted rock crystal, created by Deniot's longtime friend and collaborator Hervé Van der Straeten. The seagrass carpet—the low-key standard floor covering in French château decorating today—tones down the grandeur of the room.

In preparation for a cocktail party or dinner, Deniot often decorates the dining room table with foraged finds from the garden. One recent inspiration was branches of fragrant jasmine and Cecile Brunner roses, tangled among unmatched silver candlesticks. "I walk around the garden and find what's in season," he says. "It could be bulrushes from the stream, elderflowers, chestnut in blossom, an armful of white iris, or branches of ripe apples. I prefer it to look natural, of the moment."

For bedrooms, Deniot believes first in *douceur*, that marvelous French word that describes softness, gentleness, and comfort. He creates *douceur* with lined curtains to control sunlight, roll-down shades to adjust brightness, lights with dimmers, a bed of supreme coziness, a classic duvet, easy chairs, plus pillows (but not too many), for a sense of quiet, private repose.

In this guest room at the Chantilly house, he added a niche that cradles the head of the bed, with large closets on each side. Adjustable lights are within reach of the late-night reader. Simple carpet keeps the guest suite comfortable in summer and winter.

"I've designed bedrooms so that a guest can arrive on Friday night and quickly shower and dress for dinner. Everything is there, without fuss. Guests feel instantly at home. They can fall into bed late at night, and in summer they can leave the windows open and wake with the birds. My best advice for guest bedrooms is to make them supremely comfortable—but low-key. Lighting should be simple to adjust. And the beds are dressed simply with fresh white cotton sheets and duvet—perhaps with a baby alpaca or light Ikea wool throw."

The guest bedrooms on the second floor overlook sycamore and oak trees and acres of lawn. The eighteenth-century Swedish bed, above, is a traditional style favored for French country houses. Prints are eighteenth century. Reading lights are from the Dutch company Van Baggum Collecties. Striped wallpaper is from Farrow & Ball. Deniot built a new alcove that encloses the sleeper, with walls covered in Pierre Frey plaid cotton upholstery. Bookshelves are hidden within the niche, and there is a closet on either side.

This guest bedroom was designed in tones of pale dove gray and pale taupe. Armchairs are from Ka International. The neo-Directoire dressing table with stool in patinated wood is from 1stdibs.com. The 1940s lamp is from Baguès. Cotton shades are from Manuel Canovas. The curtains, which hang on simple wooden rods, are crafted of pale striped mattress ticking. Deniot likes to add a broad array of motifs and patterns to a tight neutral color palette, for contrast and vibrancy.

Flea-market finds give this guest bedroom suite its bohemian character. The ornate 1950s bed, painted white to tone down the baroque carving, is from the Clignancourt flea market.

Pillows were covered in velvet silk from Rubelli, and the cashmere throw is from Pierre Frey. The slightly eccentric nineteenth-century Italian canopy is dressed with silk fabric from Rubelli and cashmere from Pierre Frey. Side table lamps are from Van Baggum Collecties. The Louis XIV–style chair is covered in cotton from Pierre Frey. The whimsical Italian mirror frame in gilt wood is from the nineteenth century.

"A room can be transformed by making the best of a flea-market find," notes Deniot. This gilt wood frame was acquired with a broken mirror and then transformed into a still life with the aid of salvaged watercolor paintings, music sheets, and prints.

Children who come to Chantilly for the weekend love this bedroom. With its white quilted cotton Ralph Lauren bedspreads, antique Chinese lamp, pretty nineteenth-century bedside table, air of fantasy, and petite proportions, it pleases young tastes.

Headboards and fabric are from Ka International. Deniot notes that the simple hanging fabric canopies enhance the sense of personal space within a room and add a flourish without clutter. Continuing the blue and white theme are Chinese vases and ceramics.

The eighteenth-century gilt wood mirror (with chips left intact), marble-topped late-nineteenth-century chest of drawers, and gilt metal wall lights were all purchased during a quick early-morning swoop around Marché Serpette, the chic indoor market at Clignancourt, the oldest and largest flea market in Paris. In Deniot's fervent opinion, blue and white porcelains and blue and white fabric combinations are an absolute must in a country house.

A country kitchen, says Deniot, must be flexible, versatile, and open plan, and everything should be very accessible for weekend guests. This sunny kitchen and adjacent pantry are fitted with generous open shelves, cupboards, drawers, cabinets, and custom-designed wine storage.

The china cabinet was designed to display a hand-painted French dinnerware service (1850), originally designed for a private cruise ship on the Nile. The beadboard, painted in a pale avocado color, provides a finished backdrop for collections.

In the kitchen and pantry, pale avocado green walls reflect the garden surrounding the residence. Countertops are Bourgogne stone, and stools are from Pottery Barn. Simple curtains in cotton are from Pierre Frey. The clock, glass storage jars, and lamps are from Flamant.

Wide, accessible counter space is essential to a kitchen's convivial atmosphere, says Deniot. Here a high table was manufactured so guests can gather for *petit déjeuner*. (When there's a more formal dinner, the industrial-strength stove and worktable swing into action.)

In the evening, drinks are often served on the kitchen table or this versatile counter. A nineteenth-century birdcage creates an illusion of separation. Tall lamps in a kitchen provide a welcome disruptive element and a gleam of glamour.

DAYS OF HEAVEN

When Jean-Louis Deniot and his sister and business partner, Virginie Deniot, head to this weekend retreat in the rolling hills of Touraine, the happy escapees set out from Paris on Friday afternoons and spin southwest into another world, enticed by the promise of an idyllic country escape. It's a three-hour drive, scenic and endlessly varied. In twilight, they arrive.

The rustic eighteenth-century house, originally a farmhouse with an attic space for hay and farm implements, is surrounded by fields of wheat. In the nearest towns, weekend markets brim with the freshest fruit and vegetables, while the cheese maker fusses over his perfectly ripe regional cheeses. A winemaker sets out bottles of Vouvray and Chinon to taste.

The Deniots have created this haven with authentic and personal style. It's a place of comfort, eccentric charm, and worldly collections. Once in place, they leave only for important missions, like their local farmers' market or the many weekend *brocantes* (car boot sales, flea markets) in historic nearby towns.

It's Jean-Louis Deniot's art and craft that he effortlessly plans elegant rooms for the most luxurious art-filled Ile-de-la-Cité apartments or Ile-de-France villas—and with equal care and precision he creates his sister's farmhouse, this refuge, a family residence that comforts and inspires, and welcomes friends from around the world.

The family's menagerie seems to grow each season, and a friend observed that the weekend house is becoming more like a farm each year. They even grow their own hay.

Touraine is one of the most historic and dramatic regions of France, with the grandest chateaux and more than nine different wine appellations, including Touraine Azay-le-Rideau and Saint-Nicolas-de-Bourgueil. The countryside is unspoiled, with most acreage still agricultural.

It was in a hidden corner of the region, in an oak-framed setting, that Deniot and his sister, Virginie, found this falling-down farmhouse. The original stables were perfection, with massive ceiling beams and walls of local stone. But the buildings for the future residence were a dusty wreck.

Nonetheless, the remote location was exceptionally appealing, and Deniot immediately liked the authenticity and grit of the sheltered quadrangle, hay barns, and dirt-floored farm equipment sheds. Built in the traditional manner of terra-cotta bricks and mortar, with lichen- and moss-covered terra-cotta-tile gabled roofs, the house and outbuildings created a harmonious ensemble. The property had an expansive feeling. The brisk air smelled of ripening wheat and noble oaks.

Beneath the graceful linden tree hangs a nineteenth-century lantern found at the St.-Ouen flea market. The nineteenth-century oak table and the 1910 garden chairs were unearthed in a country antiques barn.

Following pages: The first floor of the farmhouse is essentially open from one end to the other, and rooms are delineated only by the massive old oak beams that crisscross the structure. Decorating the rooms became a frequent-flyer adventure. When Deniot was in Los Angeles for a site inspection, he picked up lamps and chairs, some at sidewalk sales, others at top showrooms. In Morocco, he found cotton and wool rugs. The coffee table was custom designed by Deniot, with an ebony stained base and oxidized hammered brass top. The glazed terra-cotta vase was purchased in Ibiza, where Deniot was working on a restoration. The eighteenth-century terra-cotta flooring was purchased on eBay and deliberately mismatched to look old and original. Sheepskins were purchased on the Isle of Skye at SkyeSkins, Scotland.

Some pieces were found just minutes from Deniot's studio in Paris. The 1840s neoclassical bas-relief is from Galerie Yves Gastou. The Argentinian throw in baby alpaca is by Eduardo Ardiles. The "Twins" tables in hammered forged steel and distressed brass are by Maryam Mahdavi, Paris. The Paradis sofa by Collection Pierre, Paris, is covered in Romo linen. A pair of lamps was made of pottery from western Germany with custom shades by Anne Sokolsky, Paris.

Deniot believes in creating decorative allegiances and visual relationships between furnishings and architectural elements. He plans harmony as well as contrast and surprise, without matching or prescribing a look. Here the black stripe on the woven cotton rug reiterates the black painted beams. Striped pillows echo the concept, but the effect is subtle.

"My plan was to keep the very rustic look, and not to 'restore' or change it much at all," says the designer. "The whole point is that it's centuries old and has great character. I wanted to keep that and to protect its integrity."

The two-story residence underwent a two-year restoration and remodel with the goal of making it look untouched. The former stable is now joined to the residence. Massive old oak beams, doubtless from the ancient forest that once carpeted France, bestow a sense of might and permanence. New floors laid with old terra cotta bricks set the style.

"I wanted to keep the interiors quite austere and not at all fancy," says Deniot, who had the new walls plastered with a traditional chalky and rough surface. He curtained the windows and doors with textured natural linen. Doors are simple oak, practical and durable.

An enfilade of rooms—with an open kitchen and dining room adjacent to a large living room, and a library/office—gives the ground floor an airy, relaxed mood.

Furnishings, art, and decorative objects came together over more than a year, as the buildings were reinforced, restored, and weatherproofed. While traveling across the globe to work with clients in India, Tangier, Miami, Long Island, Ibiza, Capri, and Caracas, Deniot always shipped back finds for the house, including fabrics, carpets, paintings, and lamps. The chaise longue was designed by Deniot and covered in BeBop fabric from Lelièvre. The dark-colored walls are punctuated with light tweed ivory drapes for brightness and verticality.

The 1950s French leather chairs with cashmere upholstery, above, are from On Site Antiques. In the living room and dining room Deniot specified traditional gritty lime paint (*peinture à la chaux*) to contribute a chalky texture and a hint of old-fashioned mystique to the walls.

Following pages: On the first floor, the solid oak beams are original to the house. The other beams were added and stained ebony to create layers and architectural dimension during renovation. The 1780s Louis XVI mantelpiece in limestone was purchased at Origines, Paris. A 1940s sunburst mirror in distressed gold leaf is from Clignancourt flea market. Deniot feels that an overscale mirror will bring a focus and point of view to a room. This bold mirror is like a ray of sunshine during the day, and it glimmers and shines in candlelight. A succession of window-adjacent rooms contributes a light-filled mood, and adds a sense of country air and relaxation, with views overlooking the fifteen-acre garden. This French enfilade concept—with doorways lined up along one side of a residence—gives a pleasing symmetry and openness to an interior.

In the kitchen/dining room, the Curtis Jere Brutalist brass lantern was found at the Fairfax flea market in Los Angeles. The custom-designed table top in tiger teakwood balances on a vintage base from Thailand. The 1940s farm chairs with straw seats from On Site Antiques were painted in khaki green by Deniot, who is never afraid to slap paint on ordinary wood furniture to freshen it up.

Chaux brossée (brushed lime paint) from Ressource Paris in Tabac Brun gives the walls an earthy appeal. Pasaya tweed fabric was used for the curtains, which hang on simple iron rods. The antique light oak display cabinet is from Philippe Colangelo, Paris. Deniot notes that reflective surfaces can contribute subtle effects to a country room with mostly matt finishes. At night, reflections of candlelight on the glass doors of the china cabinet create a romantic mood and add harmony to the composition.

Friends and family start the day, windows thrown open, with breakfast at the dining room table. The day may end with drinks around the fireplace, followed by an informal dinner. Everyone can chat to the cook.

Improvisation and invention were the order of the day for the farm's interior decoration. Avoiding every "French country" cliché, Deniot mined sources as diverse as eBay, Paris auction houses, L.A. flea markets, and Vienna sales. The quickest and most rewarding sites included the venerable Marché Paul Bert and Marché Serpette at the Clignancourt flea market, along with Ikea, chic antique shops on the Left Bank, artist friends like Hervé Van der Straeten, and the beloved country *vide-greniers* (literally "attic emptying") weekend markets that pop up in the region frequently during the summer.

"People in the region find old furniture stashed away for centuries, bring it in their car boot to a village jumble sale, and it becomes our treasure," says Jean-Louis Deniot.

The plan was for the interiors to have a comforting, solid feeling. "Over the long weekends in May, the August holidays, the family's comings and goings, country pursuits, parties, and the changing seasons, everyone can be easily and comfortably accommodated," observes Deniot. It had to be low-maintenance, with windows flung open on arrival, a Friday night dinner prepared quickly, and days spent outdoors, horseback riding or exploring nearby towns.

In summer, lunch is improvised beneath flowering linden trees, the air sweet and drowsy. Dinner is in the garden, with the last rays of golden sunlight flickering on the topmost leaves. Glasses of Chinon and excellent Vouvray from the region are poured.

In winter, shutters are closed tight, and the family gathers around blazing fires. Games of chess continue for hours. And so it will be, for many years to come.

In the kitchen, antique French demijohn glass bottles were found in the barn before renovation. The hood was custom designed by Jean-Louis Deniot in distressed, rusted steel with nail heads. The combination oven/range is by SMEG. The counters are absolute black granite. Oak cabinetry was custom designed by Deniot and painted an ebony color, with mushroom gray painted inserts. Vintage 1940 kitchen pulls were rescued from a demolition. Deniot believes that kitchen cabinets can be upgraded with a simple change of finishes and vintage hardware. Replacing hardware is intricate, but worthwhile and surprisingly effective. The Verre de Biot bottles, right, are from an auction in Normandy.

In the library, a custom bookcase in rusted metal was designed by Deniot. The 1940s sycamore armchairs by Henri Martin Etienne, in original leather, were a gift from William Randolph Hearst III when Deniot completed his Parisian apartment.

Previous pages: The whimsical console table made of salvaged elements is from Bruno Le Yaouanc, Paris. The cubic wooden coffee table from Indonesia was purchased at Art et Matières ("it weighed a ton," notes the designer). The fireplace was designed by Deniot with antique stones found during the house renovation. The eighteenth-century Louis XVI–period French trumeau, painted in the original Wedgewood blue and white, was given to Virginie and Jean-Louis by their grandmother. Deniot always avoids overdesign. Here simple oak doors were manufactured to match the wood floors.

The Napoleon III leather club chairs, trophies from an early-morning swoop through the Clignancourt flea market, have their original distressed leather. The striped rug is from Morocco. While French design is often imagined to be formal and highly codified, in reality the French traditionally praise eccentricity in design and admire the idea of English "cosy" for country décor. "The wool plaid fabric on the walls is thick and woolly, like a blanket," says Deniot.

Following pages: In the bedroom suite favored by Jean-Louis Deniot, the Indonesian king-size teak four-poster daybed, late nineteenth century, was purchased at the Tajan auction house in Paris. The custom black and emerald toile de Tours on the bedcover and matching bolsters, custom manufactured by Le Manach, is enhanced by the camouflage-style pillow fabric, a printed cotton in shades of green, black and aubergine. That yardage was a remnant from Le Manach's production for the French Air Force. (Deniot says, "I purchased the few yards they had left in their archives.") Deniot notes that a king-size bed placed sideways can be used as a deep sofa or a bed, thereby transforming an unoccupied guest room into an occasional afternoon nap room, or a casual sitting room.

To the right of the fireplace, a terra cotta neoclassical urn glazed to look like bronze stands on a base with a matching finish from Atelier Prométhée, France. A basket from Flamant holds rolled plans on tracing paper from Deniot's days as an architecture student. The Greek key cotton rug is from Williams-Sonoma. The architect's desk and chair are from Deniot's student apartment in Paris.

Above the fireplace, a backlit Curtis Jere luminous artwork was acquired in Los Angeles. The Jean-Michel Frank–style armchairs are forged iron and leather. The eighteenth-century antique gueridon is a flea market treasure. Custom beige-on-ivory herringbone-pattern toile de Tours, also by Le Manach, was used on the folding screen behind the bed. The toile was added as a large vertical stripe on the diagonal on each section of the screen to look like a herringbone pattern, adding drama and energy to the somewhat monochromatic décor. Wall upholstery in burlap fabric is from Brunschwig & Fils, with a khaki green ribbon and nail head trim finish. A pair of 1950s reading lamps by Stilnovo is from Alexandre Groult Gallery in Paris.

Following pages: The Curtis Jere–style lantern was found by the designer in a Palm Springs flea market. Pendant lights like the one above the desk are more attractive than spotlights and less predictable than standard lamps or wall sconces, Deniot suggests. A fragment of Empire-period wallpaper border by Percier et Fontaine is framed in a gold-leaf Louis XVI–period frame. The 1900 ebony display dish was brought back from a trip to Senegal, and a neoclassical ebonized 1820s round table was found in Naples, Italy. Deniot feels that a monochromatic collection in a tablescape—all-white pieces, all dark wood, all marble, all gold—makes a pleasing and harmonious grouping. Here ebony accessories on an ebony table with a black cigar box contribute depth, strength, and allure to the room.

PLAN EXISTANT
5EME ETAGE

PLAN PROJET

A collection includes an 1890 mirror from a local flea market and an eighteenth-century carved stone fragment of a horse head from Galerie Fabien Barbera, Paris.

Opposite: The stairway to the upstairs bedrooms. Amassing objects on a display shelf will animate a room and create a personal montage in an empty corner, says the designer.

In the bedroom corner, beneath hand-hewn beams, the desk, chair, and sideboard are from On Site Antiques. The 1950s Danish lamps with custom-made raffia shades are from Assemblage, Chicago. Above the desk is one of a pair of Giacometti-style blackened metal lamps, purchased in L.A.

Previous pages: In the master bedroom, walls are Pierre Frey linen fabric from Ressource, Paris, in a custom blended color. The white plaster rooster figure was crafted in 1900. Deniot believes that strong structural elements can be balanced with loose sculptural objects. The rooster contrasts with the unyielding roof beams. The Danish 1950 armchair is covered in a Rubelli fabric. The African side table is from Art & Matières. The shade fabric is "Pin Stripe" by Rubelli.

Deniot created a dramatic rustic canopy, curtains, and fringe for the bed using simple, inexpensive Brunschwig & Fils burlap with Swedish plaid from Manuel Canovas. The traditional plaid/check woven motif is echoed in the patchwork bed cover designed by Deniot in "patches" of softest alpaca from Eduardo Ardiles. The two juxtaposed scales, large and small, are visually energetic. The custom-polished brass nightstands were designed by Deniot. Wool wall-to-wall carpet is from Morocco, and the area rug is from Williams-Sonoma. The graphic custom-designed bench by Deniot with distressed bronze legs is covered in Jim Thompson "Bouclette."

Following pages: The bathroom lampshades are by Anne Sokolsky, and the lamps and mirror are from On Site Antiques. A walnut sideboard was transformed into a bathroom cabinet with a stone top. An antique buffet converted into a bathroom vanity contributes historicity, says Deniot. A Roman shade is in Colony fabric. Taps are Chambord by Cristina Ondyna, and the towel-heating rack is by Acova. The Jacob Delafon tub was painted black. A double-sloped ceiling transformed the bathroom into a bucolic heaven.

The farm-style tole-shade hanging light was a winning bid from eBay. Charming 1950 antique opaline wall lights are from On Site Antiques. The antique sink cabinet has the original Carrara marble.

Deniot says that a vintage piece can define a room's entire design. Here all the materials were chosen to match the vintage sink cabinet.

In the guest bedroom, wall upholstery in plaid fabric is from Pierre Frey. The 1880s brass twin beds were purchased in Vienna. The bed cover is in matching Romo fabric. A mahogany Louis XVI–style chest of drawers is from On Site Antiques. The ebony mirror frame is textured with nail heads. The 1950s Fornasetti-style lamp has a custom lampshade by Anne Sokolsky.

FRENCH STYLE
IN AMERICA

In Chicago, French style translates for a Francophile family to rooms and decor that suggest a mansion on the Right Bank. Jean-Louis Deniot created a dramatic iron entry door, with beveled glass glinting—a mini Hall of Mirrors. And new interior architecture, deft and perfectly proportioned, offers elegance to a 1930s apartment high above the lake. Meanwhile, in a Beverly Hills estate, a historically significant residence, designed by architect-to-the-stars Paul Revere Williams, gains luster with a fresh floor plan, a new French accent. The former maid's and chauffeur's quarters disappear, and a new pool and poolhouse make the house camera-ready. Deniot's inherent French sensibility imbues their rooms with timeless style and a new sense of design history.

LAKE VIEWS, PARIS INSPIRATIONS

Lake Michigan is distant indeed from Paris, but for one fortunate pair of Francophiles in Chicago, France is never far away.

The couple commissioned Jean-Louis Deniot to design their five-thousand-square-foot four-bedroom apartment in a prime lake-panorama location. Passionate about French design, French culture, and French art of the twentieth century, they embarked on a Paris-style idyll in Chicago, a city of great architecture and design in their home state.

"My clients, both lawyers, have had a lifelong exposure to Europe and to Paris in particular, and they have a deep and passionate understanding of centuries of French design. They were among my first clients when I was still completing architecture studies at École Camondo in Paris," recalls Deniot. He launched his career designing a charming Parc Monceau pied-à-terre for the young couple, and they continue to visit their Paris retreat often.

For the Chicago apartment, in a classical 1940s building, the couple wanted Paris salon-style references, and to highlight their art collections.

Luxurious appointments of the Chicago apartment begin at the entry, with custom-designed glass and wrought-iron doors inspired by the work of Gilbert Poillerat. The brass sunburst mirror was created by Hervé Van der Straeten. The alabaster ceiling lights are from Vaughan. Pure glamour, the custom mirrored console was designed by Deniot, inspired by the work of Serge Roche. On the console are two circa 1960 silver églomisé lamps from Assemblage, Chicago, with custom shades by Anne Sokolsky. For Deniot, custom shades are essential for an individual and luxurious polish. The striped wallpaper is from Zoffany. Custom leather and wrought-iron benches are shown to advantage on the black and gray marble floor. The painting at front left is by Moshe Rosenthalis, from the Zygman Voss Gallery in Chicago.

In the dining room, opposite, fluted plaster walls that curve up into the ceiling were designed by Deniot, inspired by an architectural Pompeii fragment he acquired in Paris. The dining table (one of two), made from ebony-stained oak with a black opaline top, was designed by Deniot and manufactured by Collection Pierre. The dining chairs, also designed by Deniot and manufactured by Collection Pierre, are upholstered in a Zimmer + Rohde horsehair and a Donghia fabric, "Debutante." The custom chandelier was designed by Deniot and made from partly gilded wrought iron and Venetian glass.

At left is a 1930s opaline urn mounted on a Macassar ebony column, originally part of the decor of the George V hotel in Paris. On the back wall is a custom bronze cabinet, designed by Deniot to accommodate the wife's superb and vivid collection of Loetz Bohemian "Tango" glass, 1918–30.

Previous pages: Deniot carved the living room from three rooms and a storage closet. The wool and silk carpet, which echoes the geometries of the new plaster ceiling, was custom designed by Jean-Louis Deniot and produced by Galerie Diurne, Paris. The slipper chairs are by Lucien Rollin. A cubist bronze and parchment coffee table was designed by Hervé Van der Straeten.

The mirrored fireplace designed by Deniot was inspired by the work of Serge Roche. Above the fireplace is an oil painting on canvas, which conceals a television. On the console table behind the sofa is a pair of bronze "Tornado" lamps created by Hervé Van der Straeten.

"I would say the original apartment, before we started work, had a very 'Park Avenue'–style floor plan, with grand living spaces, a fur coat closet, a driver's waiting room, maids' rooms, service areas for staff, and even a very large laundry where no doubt housekeepers and maids ironed linens all day and everything was top-drawer," notes Deniot. "Instead, I wanted space, light, air, and function, with clear architecture, no trickiness."

When the new construction commenced, Deniot added ceiling, wall, and molding details to give a sense of dimension. "We never do hard-core historical reconstructions or a total look," says Deniot.

After in-depth discussions with his clients in Paris and Chicago, Deniot formed an outline that included major themes of decoration from the Directoire period through the 1950s with some jolts of today. "I highlighted iconic Paris 1930s silhouettes for sofas and upholstery, updating and simplifying them, mixing them up. We make a big effort so that our effort goes unnoticed. For me, design is the art of being invisible," says the designer.

In the breakfast room, the banquette was custom designed by Deniot and manufactured by Collection Pierre. Wallpaper is by Au Fil des Couleurs, Paris. The two chrome bamboo chairs from circa 1970 are from On Site Antiques in Paris. The Warren Platner table, also circa 1970, has a black iron base and a granite top. The dog portrait, entitled *Igor,* is by François Stienne, Paris.

In Chicago, Deniot shaped cool classicism, renewing the grand traditions of French interior design and referring to such French-national-treasure designers as Jacques-Emile Ruhlmann and Jean-Michel Frank, adapted to contemporary life.

"Luxury is when it seems flawless," says Deniot. "Luxury and harmony in design happen when you reach the correct hierarchy and the perfect cohesive balance between all elements. The architecture is background, and the art is prominent. In this apartment, the collections and dramatic furniture create the excitement. Other aspects, like fabrics and carpets, needed to be quiet. Luxury is also having wall finishes, colors, lighting, side tables for drinks, paintings, collections—all in perfect harmony."

For simple, classic glamour, the bed was custom designed by Deniot and manufactured by Collection Pierre. The two Raymond Subes stools at the end of the bed are from Malmaison in New York. The 1940s Baguès chandelier is from Douglas Rosin in Chicago. A Ruhlman design inspired the custom wool rug by Galerie Diurne, Paris. The "Marla" bedside chest is part of a furniture collection Deniot designed for Collection Pierre, in black lacquer and brass, with an opaline top. A pair of Murano glass lamps dates from the 1960s, with custom Anne Sokolsky shades.

Above: The carved and gilded 1960s coffee table is by Phyllis Morris. The Macassar ebony and brass-inlay television cabinet was designed by Deniot. The pair of celadon crackled-glaze ceramic vases on giltwood bases is from Monument, San Francisco.

The starting point for the design of the library was the Ruhlmann fabric on the two Austrian art decor armchairs, purchased in Budapest. The fabric is a special color run created by Prelle. The vintage green malachite coffee table by Maison Jansen was purchased from Galerie Lalbatry. On the table is a 1922 Loetz candy dish, and on the wall is a 1945 Serge Poliakoff painting. The Jean-Michel Frank sofa is upholstered in a Larsen mohair velvet, with a pillow in Rubelli fabric. The stained oak bookcase was designed by Deniot, as was the silk and Nepalese wool Diurne rug. The glass table lamps were purchased from Assemblage, with custom shades by Anne Sokolsky.

Opposite: Deniot discovered the 1970s Phyllis Morris bed at Assemblage in Chicago and had it lacquered black. Pillows on the bed are made from a toile de Tours by Georges Le Manach. The bed cover is made from a Brunschwig & Fils fabric. A pair of fantasy tables was designed by Ruben de Saavedra. On the wall is a rug cartoon by Claude Bleynie for Aubusson from the 1940s. The custom rug was designed by Deniot and made by Galerie Diurne.

HOLLYWOOD CLASSIC, FRENCH TRANSLATION

J ean-Louis Deniot acquired a residence in Los Angeles a decade ago, and since then he has immersed himself in the vivid cultural and social life of this vibrant and glamorous city.

Recently he secured an elegant house overlooking Beverly Hills, designed in 1938 by the noted architect-to-the-stars, Paul R. Williams. In the golden age of cinema, Williams created residences for such stars as ZaSu Pitts, Luise Rainer, and Frank Sinatra.

The house, surrounded by a pretty garden, had been beautifully maintained but needed a subtle update, a modified floor plan, and new amenities. Deniot conducted research on Williams's signature style, and then brought his inherent French sensibility to the interiors. With a one-year remodel, he created a series of cohesive rooms that are California-light and fresh, with a subtle Paris perfume.

Today a whiff of Jean-Michel Frank drifts in the air. A dream-sequence color palette of pale taupe, ivory, sand, off-white, and pale grays offers a soothing backdrop with a pronounced French accent.

Deniot spent months planning and a year reshaping the 1938 house, adding new terraces, editing extraneous details in the entry, restyling the pool house, and enhancing every corner of the interiors. He reconfigured the 4,500-square-foot layout, carving out five bedroom/bathrooms with artful new schematics. His goal was not to modernize it or reinvent it, but to unify the details with a confident sense that the house had not been touched.

In the entry hall, above, is a 1940s Maison Jansen coral lacquered desk. The ceramic lamp is 1950s, and the resin stool is by Claudio Salocchi, 1970.

Juxtaposed with the modulated wall colors are a series of sculptural Vladimir Kagan sofas, graphic new work by contemporary Los Angeles artists, super-charged African artifacts, custom-made Nepalese rugs designed by Deniot, chic Maison Jansen treasures, and the airiest raw silk curtains.

"My goal was for the original architecture to stand out, so that it is not evident where I actually altered elements," says Deniot. "I worked with Paul Williams always in mind, as if he was still making the decisions. I have high respect for his architecture. I then implemented the decor with all my European influences, which suited the house style perfectly."

The goal was to protect the original elegant aesthetic but also to show in a very subtle way its Hollywood heritage.

"I certainly did not want a full-on Hollywood Regency look, which is fun, but not the look I wanted," says Deniot. "I did not want midcentury. I played with my own influences—French, neo-classical, along with vintage American classics—trying to achieve the perfect balance between style, history, and contemporary living." Once the canvas of the architecture was prepared, I added my version of how a Paul Williams house should look today."

The living room is in effect a grand salon. With a Vladimir Kagan sofa in the bay window, a chaise longue, and comfortable chairs, it has versatile seating for many occasions, Deniot notes. "I wanted to create interesting interactions and perspectives for all guests. The new Jean de Merry day bed was added for maximum attitude, and other pieces play contrasts between sharp and loose, precise and organic shapes."

The custom Nepalese wool rug in the living room was designed by Deniot, as was the Jean de Merry XXL marble, bronze, and parchment console. Obelisks are bronze. The large, abstract painting is by Claudia Aronow-Roush.

Previous pages: A 2013 Jean de Merry gray parchment daybed is covered in abstract silk damask. The coffee table is onyx, and the armchair and stool are by T. H. Robsjohn-Gibbings. In the bay window is a Vladimir Kagan sofa. Floor lamps are 1950 Jacques Adnet, and the long Edward Wormley sofa covered in alpaca is from Loro Piana.

Deniot knew that houses designed by Paul Revere Williams attracted generations of stars—Lucille Ball and Desi Arnaz, and actor Jack Oakie—all with limited exposure to European classical architecture but with daily familiarity to the fantasy decor of film. Williams could sketch and plan light interpretations of popular French Regency and French country, as well as varied Mediterranean vernacular architecture (there are suggestions of all three in this house). Today his work is highly desirable to L.A. real estate connoisseurs.

In the master bedroom, the custom Nepalese rug was designed by Deniot. The bed has a Hollywood Regency–style faux bamboo headboard. The parchment console is by Karl Springer. A 1940 French Maison Carlhian sofa is covered in Loro Piana cashmere. The Brutalist coffee table is by Daniel Gluck, and chairs are by Harvey Probber.

Previous pages: In the dining room, Deniot added neoclassical columns and floor-to-ceiling trumeaux with antique mirror glass. The Jean de Merry custom dining table has a bronze base and matte lacquered top. Eight 1950s dining chairs were recovered. Consoles are by Emilio Terry, and the girandole lamps are Directoire style.

The balustrade on the landing is original. A Jean de Merry collection console has gold-leaf forged iron legs, and a parchment top was designed by Deniot.

In a bay window at one side of the kitchen, Deniot created a congenial morning room, with a circular leather-clad table and Kipp Stewart chairs. A Swedish portrait is from the eighteenth century. For fantasy, there's a 1930s beaded chandelier.

In contrast to the detail and kinetic movement of the house, the new kitchen is rather understated and classical. The old kitchen was taken down to the studs, and re-created as an idealized classical kitchen, in keeping with the period of the house. "It's very well-equipped but not intended to be a design statement," says Deniot.

One of the most luxurious (and essential) additions to the house was the swimming pool, now updated and restyled, with a handsome stone terrace. Deniot designed this setting with lots of privacy and shade, as well as a series of comfortable seating groups. In the pool house, above, the large Curtis Jere fish sculpture, Willy Daro coffee table, and Stiffel bronze lamps work perfectly in homage to the original period of the house, and the almost film-set-style elegant aspirations of Beverly Hills residential decor.

INSIDE THE MIND AND METHOD OF JEAN-LOUIS DENIOT

IN CONVERSATION WITH DIANE DORRANS SAEKS

Jean-Louis Deniot has always embraced collaboration with decorative artists, sculptors, woodcarvers, plasterers, painters, rug weavers, furniture manufacturers, and many other talents.

Here he reveals his love and respect for the creative talents he works with, and their essential role in crafting personal, lasting, and highly individual rooms.

SOURCES

Each interiors project presents a specific, individual point of view and reflects the requirements and life of my clients over decades. Ethically and aesthetically I never repeat a design. I use mostly antique or one-of-a-kind vintage accessories and furniture, and I custom design everything else. This way I achieve a very specific result, which is unique to each project and each client.

I am very loyal to my favorite vendors, and I enjoy the working relationship and the ongoing product development we share. I've been working for many years with the Paris-based carpet company, Diurne. The quality of their handmade carpets is very fine, and they approach each project in an artistic manner. I consider their rugs like floor art. They pull everything together as an ideal backdrop.

For each rug design, I consider the balance of color, pattern, and contrast throughout the room, elaborating a strong or a very muted rug design depending on whether it needs to be predominant or just a soft backdrop. I custom design every rug for all projects (except for some spectacular antique floor coverings). I work mostly with Gallerie Diurne and Gallerie Solstys. They custom make the rugs in Nepal in pure wool and sometimes silk blend or accents.

ANTIQUES AND VINTAGE

Jane Alexander, an antiques and sourcing specialist, is responsible for our antiques and vintage department. She works closely with her assistant, Caroline Bonnetti, to collect a broad array of pieces from around the world. Jane and Caroline travel regularly to Brussels, New York, Milan, London, Los Angeles, Denmark, Berlin, and Stockholm, as well as to dealers in Paris. They check special sites online and have excellent auction contacts.

Each project tells a story, so each search has very specific requirements. Jane works with my storyboard, with all the information on a new project and its style. My outline has a very detailed furniture layout, with all items numbered to define art, antiques, and decorative objects, and which pieces will be custom made. I create visuals of the pieces I have in mind, to help Jane create the link between all elements. Sourcing the right scale is the most important point. My work is all about perfect scale, and Jane knows the exact dimensions and quality.

CUSTOM

Two specialists on staff are responsible all year long for the many custom designs I specify. We manufacture custom designs all over the world, including mother-of-pearl from India, hammered brass and silver from Morocco, parchment and shagreen from the Philippines, mirrors, tables, embroideries, and embellishments.

Special crafts are also sourced in France—such as Lison de Caunes for straw marquetery, *églomised* glass work by Florence Girette, abstract hand-painted silk by Petra, bronze or raffia—and I often select exceptional silk embroidery work by Jean-François Lesage. I enjoy working with weavers, parquet layers, stonemasons, marble sculptors, and many others.

NEW LIMITED-EDITION DESIGNS

One signature of my work is the use of many limited-edition artist pieces. I often work closely with Hervé Van der Straeten to custom craft pieces from his collections. He creates large-scale mirrors, lamps, sculptures, finials, or chandeliers, depending on the challenges and requirements. I love his variations on sculptural mirrors and find that his new chandeliers give eighteenth-century rooms a quick jolt. It is all about the right amount of art, lighting, and drama, the right balance: *l'equilibre*.

I work with a number of artists and have commissioned pieces by Guy de Rougemont, Mattia Bonetti, Manuela Zervudachi, and many others in India, Morocco, Los Angeles, and New York. This is one of the great pleasures of my work, and for my clients it is exciting to have a one-of-a-kind chandelier, bedroom mirror, sculpture, or furniture piece.

FURNITURE AND METAL LINES

In France since 2006 I have produced three complete lines with Collection Pierre, which now number about one hundred pieces.

I enjoy this manufacturer, as they have been crafting furniture for almost a century, including for such designers as Jean-Charles Moreux, Emile-Jacques Ruhlmann, Jean Royère, Maison Jansen, and André Arbus.

My collection for Bronze d'art de France celebrates the tradition of *bronze de style*, from Louis XV, Empire, and Louis XVI. I designed contemporary styles and lines entirely in bronze, including coffee tables, side tables, reading lamps, wall lights, and chandeliers.

For Pouenat Ferronnier, a traditional metalwork house, I introduced lines in 2012 and 2014. Like a private designer's club, Pouenat carries lines by India Mahdavi, Gilles et Boissier, and Damien Langlois-Meurinne.

I designed a line of outdoor furniture for MyMaille, mostly for the rare property and yachting market. Entirely clad with outdoor leather, it's faux bamboo, to bring the sophistication of indoor finishes in outdoor environments.

In the UK, since 2010 I've produced a line with Marc de Berny called Sparkx, including coffee tables, side tables, dressing tables, and mirrors. They are modern, like fireworks—all very happy. Also in the UK, a new line with George Smith has high-quality upholstery with dining chairs, sofas, and armchairs in an updated traditional style.

In Russia, I designed the new Modenature collection. The line is my most contemporary, with sleek lines, leather, darker wood in high gloss, or textured wood finishes.

In the U.S., I designed a line for Jean de Merry, taking advantage of his exquisite finishes, parchment, shagreen, bronze, *églomised* glass, bronze, and rock crystals. I am very proud that the largest and most widely distributed line will be for Baker furniture. It is a very exciting seventy-piece line, including lighting, furnishing, and accessories, and will be released in 2015.

FABRICS

Our office has four specialists/decorators sourcing from every vendor. We work most often with the decades-old French company Le Manach, as well as Jim Thomson, Sabina Fay Braxton, Pierre Frey, Rubelli, Donghia, and many others, buying literally miles of fabrics every year. We source rare, one-of-a-kind, handcrafted, and limited-edition fabrics during trips, and we visit fabric markets in New Delhi and Jaipur, shipping materials back from India to Paris.

Sometimes fabrics are sourced in Paris at the great Marché St. Pierre. This is a historic market selling out-of-season fabrics, excellent simple basics (canvas, muslin), and leftover yardage such as cashmere, tweeds, raffia, handmade African fabrics, and Indian embroideries.

In Los Angeles and New York I shop at Mood fabrics, a very inspiring warehouse that carries mostly fashion fabrics—the type of product you could never find in interior collections. You can buy one-off Loro Piana baby alpaca tweed yardage, Marc Jacobs wool and cashmere, and painted denims by Carolina Herrera

In Morocco I go to the fondouks in Tangier to buy small yardage of handwoven fabrics in wool and cotton. I custom manufacture many unique designs, playing with specific techniques, textures, and updated color palettes. Also in Tangier, Morocco, I'm very fond of Majid, who has a superbly curated selection of antique textiles, antiques, beads, and curious objects. His collection is like a museum, and he is a treasure.

THE MOST VERSATILE, BASIC FABRIC

There is always natural linen, of course, and wool tweed. But for real versatility, I frequently use "Toile de Tours" by Georges Le Manach. It is in thick, woven cotton that is very dry and also slightly spongy. The interesting aspect of this material is that you can partially customize it by using one of fifty available patterns woven with your own color palette. The pattern can range from traditional, textured, or contemporary. It is so versatile that it can be used in every project yet never look the same.

NEW TEXTILES I LOVE

Sabina Fay Braxton's hand-printed fabric collections are so creative, using ancient techniques that can be rustic or very lavish and rich. They feature rough cotton bases, soft textured chenille with abstract motifs and bronze accents, silk velvet, rich colors, often mysteriously beautiful. Super-chic. They work equally as well on a Louis XVI armchair as they would on a Vladimir Kagan sofa.

PAINT

Color straight from the can is not for me. Custom mixes are precisely what I want. Depending on natural light, the same color in two different locations won't look the same. I prefer to adapt the shades to each site. Ressource in Paris is probably the best paint you can buy worldwide. The color palettes are superb, from the historic to current collections. The quality, texture, and richness of pigment give substantial depth to any wall or surface. I often use paint from the *couleurs historiques* collection by Ressource. It is very heavily pigmented and the best quality I know. It's very thick, and the brushstrokes remain visible after application. The result is very deep, just like an Yves Klein monochrome. I love all shades of gray, blues, greens, pinks, and taupes.

In the U.S. Benjamin Moore has a great line of products too. In the UK I use Paint Library, Chelsea, with 340 fabulous colors, heavy pigmented, the absolute best English paint.

HARDWARE

This is a very important final touch on all elements of interior architecture, and I work most often with Maison Schmidt in Paris, as they still manufacture the highest level of quality finishes. I enjoy their historic selection from the Régence period, Louis XVI, Directoire, Ruhlmann, Dupré-Lafon, Jansen, and Arbus. They have all original hardware and molds from these periods, as well as specific custom designs.

FAVORITE RESTAURANT/CAFE IN PARIS

Bistro de Paris on the rue de Lille anytime. It's near my office, and I know everyone. Sometimes I go as often as four times a week. It is a very traditional French bistro with great seasonal food, old-Paris atmosphere, good service, and nice owners.

FAVORITE PLACE FOR AN ESCAPE

When I discovered Tangier, Morocco, I decided that it is pure paradise. No wonder Yves Saint Laurent spent half his life there, escaping Paris as often as possible. I have acquired a property there, with sea views and a large lush garden. It's quiet, located outside town. I've designed lighting, carpets, fabrics, and furnishings that are being made by local craftsmen. I'm also very fond of India and want to spend more time exploring. It's endlessly fascinating, with rich culture and history.

ON MY IPOD

I have very eclectic taste in music. It changes. I have some soul, Nina Simone "My Baby Just Cares for Me," some classical music, Bach "Prelude and Fugue in C Major," some electro pop, Empire Under the Sun's "Walking on a Dream," some Indian music, Appa's "Badmarsh and Shri," some more electro, The Asteroids Galaxy Tour's "Push the Envelope," and finally "Fireworks" by my dear friend Katy Perry.

FAVORITE FILM AND TELEVISION

Les Liaisons Dangereuses, obviously. The decor, costumes, production colors, actors, makeup, candles, and period furnishing make it such a beautiful picture.

My favorite TV show is *Mad Men*. The look of the show and the characters are gorgeous. The sets and decor are stylish. It's very pleasing to watch such a fun period/era so well created. I often watch it in L.A., and sometimes in Paris. It has focus, style, and the exactitude of creating a time, a place, a look.

MOST INSPIRING DESIGN BOOKS

I have two interior design bibles: *Architecture Intérieure et Décoration en France des Origines à 1875* by Jean Feray and *Les Décorateurs des Années 40* by Bruno Foucart and Jean-Louis Gaillemin. My library continues to grow as I add definitive monographs. Among my sources for design books are Galignani and Karl Lagerfeld's 7L bookshop on rue de Lille in Paris. And I love finding faded old design books, by chance, at country flea markets, at Clignancourt, and in Los Angeles sidewalk sales.

NEWEST DESIGN DISCOVERIES

I admire the abstract patterns by embroidery company Jean-François Lesage. These are amazing embroidered textures with wool, bronze, cotton, and silk. We have worked on projects with hand-painted silk wallpapers and embroidery by Fromental and custom rugs by Fort Street Studio on Broadway in New York City.

THANK YOU.
MERCI BEAUCOUP.

Directing and writing *Jean-Louis Deniot Interiors* has been a voyage of discovery, across continents and centuries of style and design. Thank you, Jean-Louis, for three profoundly inspiring years working with you on this wonderful monograph. The logic, clarity, emotion, history, elegance, and harmony of your architecture and interiors continue to be inspiring and uplifting.

It has been the greatest pleasure to get inside the vivid and disciplined mind of Jean-Louis Deniot. I admire his extraordinary talent, and his fierce and constant drive to create beauty.

I met Jean-Louis when he was a young architecture student, even before he founded his global company in 2000, and have always admired his intense focus on design. I've encountered his clients (a highly accomplished global group who adore him) and watched the triumph of his international career in architecture and design.

Rizzoli publisher Charles Miers championed this book and gave me the freedom and structure to craft a richly illustrated, informational, and rare book. This is my seventh book for Rizzoli. Charles's guidance and insight are greatly valued. My editor, Alexandra Tart, is my objective viewpoint, so truly valuable and appreciated. I admire Alex's refined eye, her meticulous elegance, her focus, and her "hands-off" approach to my writing. Working with her has been an extraordinary privilege and pleasure.

At team Rizzoli, I have worked closely for many years with the great Pam Sommers, the executive director of publicity, and the wonderful Jessica Napp, associate director of publicity. They are utterly efficient and creative, the best of the best. It is my great pleasure to work with Pam, Jessica, and their team. Dung Ngo has always been a favorite editor, insightful and deeply involved in the worlds of architecture, design, and style.

This is my seventh book with art director Paul McKevitt and his team at Subtitle, New York. Each book has its own character, integrity, and mojo. I have great respect for Paul's polished and graceful professionalism and exceptional style. Thank you, Paul.

To Xavier Béjot, whose elegant and polished photography illuminates the book, I send my warmest thanks and admiration. Xavi, merci beaucoup pour ces images, belles et émotionelles.

To the fabulous Deniot team at rue de Verneuil headquarters, thank you for your dedication, style, and passion. Virginie Deniot expertly directs the Jean-Louis Deniot studio. Superb. Patricia de Oliviera and Susannah Maund have worked meticulously to collate materials for this book. Their professionalism as the "Paris branch" of my office is sincerely appreciated. Jane Alexander was exceptionally helpful with antique dealers, art galleries, and sources.

In particular, I would like to thank my longtime friend William Holloway for first introducing Jean-Louis to me. William, living in Paris at the time, identified the brilliant talent of Jean-Louis and saw his rare discipline and knowledge. Merci, William.

As always, hurtling onward into the constant now. With thanks.

DIANE DORRANS SAEKS

ACKNOWLEDGMENTS

I dedicate this book to Virginie Deniot, Montaine Desouches, Jane Alexander, and William Holloway.

I would like to address my warmest thanks first to Diane Dorrans Saeks for her creativity, exceptional insight, support, and trust.

I extend my special thanks to Alexandra Tart, Paul McKevitt, Charles Miers, Pam Sommers, and Xavier Béjot for their invaluable work and exceptional involvement. Without all of them, none of this would have been possible.

My thanks go to: Ingrid Abramovitch, Jean-Jacques Aillagon, Princess Paula Al-Sabah, Rumaan Alam, Charles Albessard, Elaine Alexander, Jane Alexander, Elina Alexandrova, Kira Alves, Laurent Apigalli, Eduardo Ardiles, Paola Arigoni, Philippe Aubry, Mr. and Mrs. and Thibault Audenet, Suzanne Augostino, Ria & Youri Augousti, Jérôme Aumont, Hervé Austin, M. Avner, Chris Bagley, Glen Ballard, Rodolphe Banier et Stéphanie Ovadia, Sara Banti, Santiago Barberi, Natasha Barbier, Dr. Barel, Mrs. Barel, Amit Barel, Neil Barrett, Baukje Beetsma, David Bensoussan, Emmanuel Berard, Harold Berard, Gabriel Bernardi, Véronique Berthelot, Heidy Betz, Alexandre Biaggi, Anita Bijlsma, Princess Mashael Bint Sultan, Irina Birilova, Dmitri Birukov, Laurent Blanc, Clémence Blanchard, Martine Blanck Dap, Marie-Claire Blanckaert, Frank Blard, Franca Boccoli, Céline Bogureau, Jean Bond Rafferty, Mattia Bonetti, Caroline Bonetti, Marc and Munira Bonnet de Berny, Michael Boodro, Theresa Boyed, Tamsin Bradshaw, Rémy Brazet, Etienne Breton, Philippe Brugidou, Sophie Brunet, Michael Bruno, Rita Caltagirone, Yves Carcelle, Jules Caris, Ernie Carswell, Florence Cervoni, Jérôme Chanvillard, Jason Chen, Alena Cherepanova, Polina Chesova, Angelica Cheung, Christian Chevassus, Sylvain, Mireille and Antoine Chevanne, Doris Chevron, Marie Christophe, Clare Churly, Ruth Clapper, David Clark, Emmanuel et Laetitia Collini, David Collins, Jonn Coolidge, Valerie Cortenraede, Helena Couffin, Anne Crawford, Jamie Creel and Marco Scarani, Susan Crewe, Gaëtan D'Hôtel, Jonas Dahl, Sandy and Julie Dalal, Gilles Dalliere, Christian Darnaud-Maroselli, Agnès Darricau, Victoria Davydova, Sylvie de Chirée, Virginie de la Battut, Princess Diane de Beauvau-Craon, Princess Laure de Beauvau-Craon, Princess Minnie de Beauvau-Craon, Lison de Caunes, Isabel de La Chica, Bruno de Caumont, Eric de Dormael, Chantal de Galbert, Sylvie de Lattre, Jean de Merry, José De Oliveira, Patricia De Oliveira, Rose Anne de Pampelonne, Portia de Rossi, Siki de Somalie, Ramuntcho De Saint Amand, Ellen DeGeneres, Jerome and Michèle Delemer, Xavier Delesalle, Francesco Della Femina, Béatrice Delon, Edouard Demachy, Gérard and Michelle Deniot, Dominique Deniot, Simone Deniot, Virginie Deniot, Montaine Desouches, Julien Desouches, Jacqueline Develay, Gilles Dewavrin, Jim Dixon, Aleksey Dorozhkin, Shirley Doukhan, Stephen Drucker, Mr. and Mrs Heriard Dubreuil, Jean-Hugues Dumont, Antoine Dumortier (Solstys), Valerie Duport, Laura Duque, Giles Ellwood, Carolyn Englefield, Cinzia Felicetti, Adine Fichot, Vitor Figueiredo, Miguel Flores-Vianna, Cliff Fong, Agnès Forcade, Melonie Foster Hennessy, Ariel Foxman, Jane Francisco, Cynthia Frank, Julia Freemantle, Pierre, Lorraine, Vincent, Matthieu and Patrick Frey, Bruno Frisoni, Nina Garcia, Diego Garcia Scaro, Yves et Victor Gastou, Claire Gauthier, Laina Gianferrari, Flavia Giorgi, Florence Girette, Serge Gleizes, Pamela Golbin, Victoria Gomez Día, Nancy Gonzalez, Wendy Goodman, Emilio Gottardo, Emma Grigoryeva, Alexandre Groult, Sushant Gupta, Rachel Hardage Barrett, Sarah G. Harrelson, John Hart, William R. Hearst III, Bernard Henriot, Mary Hessing, Donelle Higbee, Analuz Holloway, Anthony Holloway, William Holloway, David Hopkins, Betsy Horan, Melanie Horcholle, Angela Hudson and Svend Lerche, Alexandra Hughes, Lilian Ingenkamp, Elena Ivanova, Oliver Jahn, Eric Jansen, Amod Jha, Jaime Jimenez, Fabrice Juan, Stephan Julliard, Marie Kalt, Elena Kananykina, Mr. and Mrs. Kendall, Kevin and Karen Kennedy, Rajeev Khanna, Valeriya Kholodova, Kika, Mathias Kiss, Robert Klingel, Rachel Kohler, George Kotsiopoulos, David, Anouck, Sandra et Daniel Koskas, Jean Kremer, Maria Kryzhanovskaya, Lucien La, Valter La Tona, Murray Lappe, Parker Larson, Guillaume Le Gall, Bruno Le Yaouanc, Mr. and Mrs. Leach, Aurélie Leblanc, Stéphane Lecoq, Nathalie Lemaire, Robert Lemarié, Fabrice Léonard, Jean-François Lesage, Bruno Levesque, Audrey Levine, Jeff Locker, Véronique Lopez, Olga Lopez, Cynthia Lund, Marie-Hélène Lundgreen, Princess Masha Magaloff, Maryam Mahdavi, Jeff Marcus, Kathryn Marx, Neharika Mathur Sinha, Susannah G. Maund, Mary McDonald, John McNamara, Ellie S. McNevin, Sarah Medford, Eugenia Mikulina, Jennifer Mitchell, Léo Mogas, Mia Moretti, Cédric Morisset, Liz Morris, Carlos Mota, Gladys Mougin, James Nauyok, Kathy Nelson, M. Nicolas Hamel, Sheila Nielsen, Helena Nimbratt, Natalia Obukhova, Michelle Ogundehin, Natalia Onufreichuk, Annabel Osbourne, Philippe Ouellet, Stephanie Paas, Anne-Sophie Pailleret, Florentino Pamintuan, Tatiana Pankova, Manuelle Papapietro, Enric Pastor, Delphine Pastor, Annie Pate, Charles Patterson, Jane Pendry, Katy Perry, Julia Peshkova, Simon Pesin, Gilles and Elliott Petiot, Jean et Madeleine Petiot, Svetlana Petrova, Ian Phillips, Olivier Piel, François and Maryvonne Pinault, Anna Polyushkoa, Carlo Ponti, Richard Powers, Alexandre Pradère, Isabelle and Cyrille Proutchenko, Serge Proutchenko, Simone Quintas, Moin, Nasreen, Pernia and Sylvia Qureshi, Manju Rajan, Carole et Jacques Rayet, Kate Reardon, Susan Rerat, Michel Richard, Cédric Riou et Benôit Ruffenach (Atelier Prométhée), Alice Ritter, Mallery Roberts, Whitney Robinson, Alix-Marie Roblot, Florence Rogers, Anastasia Romashkevich, Francis Roos, Amelie Roux, Robert Rufino, Margaret Russell, Alexandra Rymkevich, Cédric Saint André Perrin, Lay-lah Salie, Marco Sandrini, Alexandra Sarramona, Hakan and Aylin Sarihan, Saro Family, Anita Sarsidi, Jean-Charles Saudemont, Paolo Scarani, Stephen Schaffer, Janie Schaffer, David Schwartz, Emily Senior, Béatrice Serre, Natalia Shkuleva, Timon Sinclair, Clinton Smith, Audrey Snauwaert, Anne Sokolsky, Olga Sorokina, Julia Stern, Tim Street-Porter, Catherine Sullivan, Natalie Sutton, Iris Tang, Jean-Louis Tapiau, Roustam Tchingariev, Tatiana Telegina, Jacqueline Terrebonne, Sylvie Thébaud, Anne-Cécile Thirifays, Rupert Thomas, Jade Thomson, Glenn, Gayle and Rebecca Tilles, Natalia Timasheva, Stefano Tonchi, Mireille Tracol, Gilles Trillard, Newell Turner, Leyla Uluhanli, Simon Upton, Jonny Valiant, Hervé Van Der Straeten, Thomas Vasseur, Christopher and Alison Viehbacher, Claude Vieillard, Eric Vincent, Brian Vytlacil, Chris Wade, Samir Wadekar, Ekaterina Wagner, Heather Walter, Yuki Wang, Xu Wang, François Warnot, Katie Watson Smyth, Kelly Wearstler, Neale Whitaker, Kelli Wilde and Laurent Champeau, Faye Wisberg, Su Yan, Sean Yashar, Caroline Young, Marcel Zelmanovitch (Diurne), Jasmin Zetlmeisl, Irina Zhuravleva, Yury Zinkin

—JEAN-LOUIS DENIOT